"Free"
Letters and Remembrances of Vietnam with a selection of Civil War letters written by Eugene Kingman

by

Andrew L. Phelan

Photographs and drawings by the author

Design by Lei Cai

Cover Design by Larry Burditt

ISBN (10) 0-9788570-0-3

2006
Quail Creek Editions
1811 Quail Creek Drive
Norman, Oklahoma 73026
© All rights reserved.

No portion of this book may be reproduced without the written permission of the author

No part of this publication may be reproduced, stored in a retrieval system or transmitted in any form electronic or otherwise or by any means without the prior permission of the author.

"Free"

*Letters and Rememberances of Vietnam with a selection of
Civil War letters written by Eugene Kingman*

by Andrew L. Phelan

Quail Creek Editions
1811 Quail Creek Drive
Norman, Oklahoma 73026

2006

© All rights reserved. No part of this publication may be reproduced, stored in a retrieval system or transmitted in any form electronic or otherwise or by any means without the prior permission of the author.

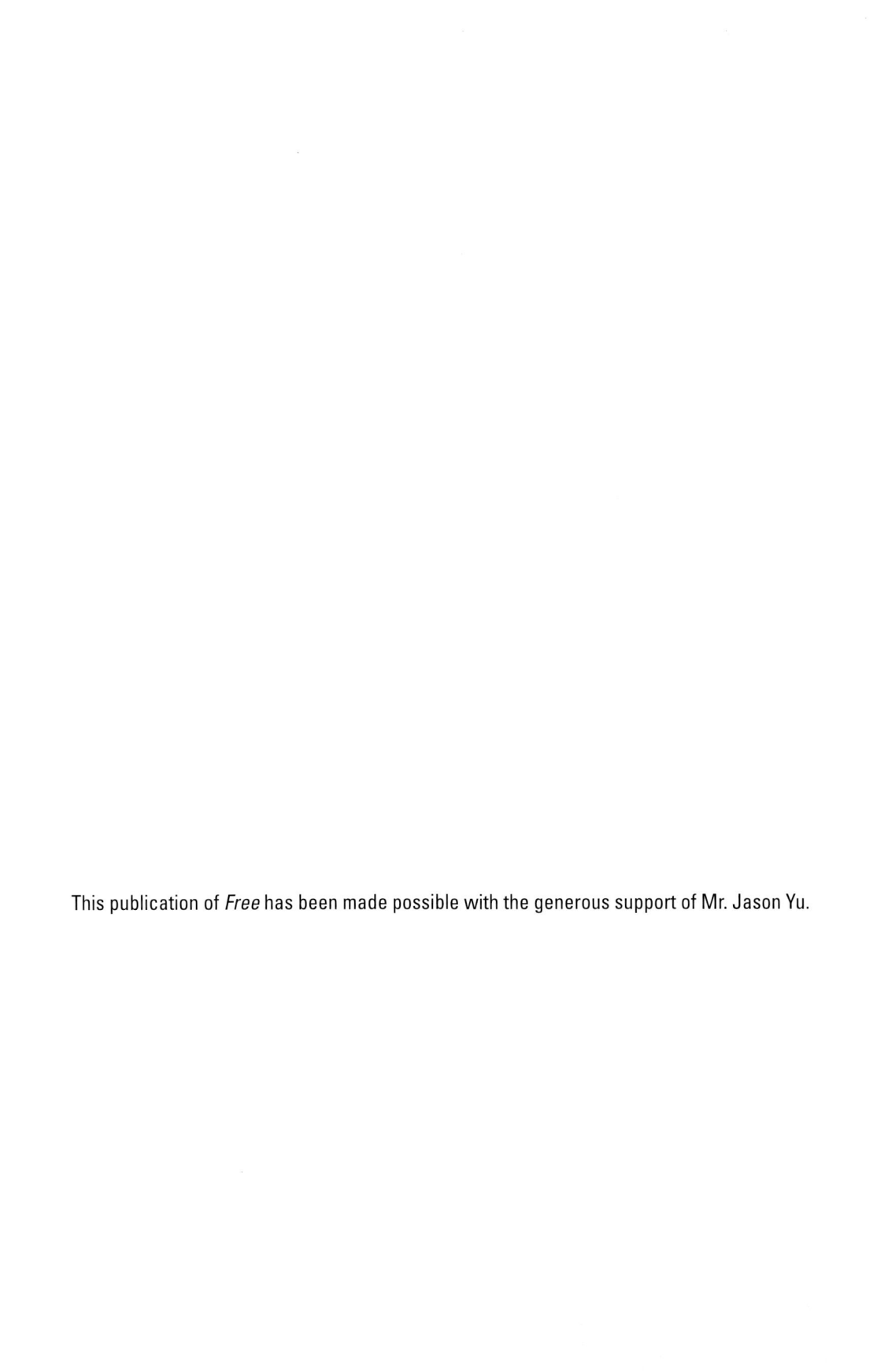

This publication of *Free* has been made possible with the generous support of Mr. Jason Yu.

Preface

This book is a personal account of my time in Vietnam in 1969 and 1970. It grew out of the surprise discovery in 1997 that my letters home to my parents, my grandmother and my sister had survived. Also surviving were a couple of letters to the Robert Turners, family friends.

For more than a quarter of a century following my return from Vietnam, I had assumed that my letters had disappeared along with that part of my life. But suddenly, there they were tied together in bundles and still in the envelopes marked "free". (Soldiers serving in Vietnam did not have to use postage stamps. If you had a Vietnam APO address, all you had to do was write "free" in the upper right hand corner of the envelope where a stamp was usually placed.)

When I came back from Vietnam, I made a conscious decision to put the experience behind me, determined to focus on my personal future and its possibilities, not dwell on the past. I should add that, in retrospect, this decision was almost mandatory because, as an artist and professor in the visual arts living in New York City, no one wanted to hear about my Vietnam service. Indeed, for the first few years most of my professional colleagues made no bones about the fact that they considered anyone who had served to be more or less politically suspect and lacking in moral character. Maintaining collegial relationships made it almost mandatory for me never to discuss the issue.

So, for years, I rarely spoke about Vietnam, although I do remember that shortly after we were married, my then-wife asked me if I had any photographs from Vietnam, and I arranged a slide show one night. I also talked a bit about it with my sister-in-law's husband who had served in the Marines and had spent time in Lebanon. But not talking about it much wasn't too hard since there weren't many of my professional or personal friends who had served in Vietnam. (Indeed, for most of my life it has been very rare to find a colleague or friend who had shared the Vietnam experience.)

After the letters appeared, I read them. Needless to say, it is very interesting to re-open a window to your past in such an unexpected way. Having done so, the next step was to decide what, if anything, I wanted to do with them!

The answer came to me after a trip to New York City in April 1998. While there, I made a pilgrimage to the New York Vietnam Veterans Memorial, which, in the early 1980's I had the privilege of helping to bring into reality as a member of the New York Vietnam Veterans Committee. With rain coming down under a menacing sky and with helicopters making a familiar racket while taking off from the Downtown Heliport across the East Side Drive, I stood for a few minutes and looked at the darkened Monument bereft of its pools of water and barren of any offerings or admiring glances. There was no one else around on this dark, dreary and rainy morning, so I stood, quietly thoughtful and reflective - and alone.

I remembered the dedication ceremonies in 1983, replete with festivities, a ticker tape parade down Broadway, spectacular fireworks off Battery Park and a splendid evening of dining and dancing at Trump Tower in Midtown Manhattan - and enormous cheering crowds. That evening, when we dedicated the Memorial and the switch was thrown illuminating the translucent wall with its engraved quotations of words from the letters home, the crowd gave a collective gasp in appreciation and wonder - and then cheered wildly. The celebration and the tickertape parade that followed were a far cry from the initial reception that I and most Vietnam veterans got when they returned home to a largely indifferent and sometimes hostile populace. There were no victory parades, no days put aside as a national holiday, for remembrance. The Monument was an effort to counter that neglect.

But the attention paid to the Monument and veterans rapidly dissipated and, by the time I visited, had all but disappeared.

So, on this morning, only the sound of the helicopters and of the ever-present East River Drive traffic droned on as I stood, looking at the forlorn memorial, dark and lightless - stripped of its dignity but not of its evocative power.

On the top of one of the walls, filled with quotes from letters home, there is etched a quote from a letter sent in 1968 by then Lt. J. G. Strandberg to his wife: *"One thing worries me - will people believe me? Will they want to learn about it, or will they want to forget the whole thing happened?"* (The full letter is quoted in *Dear America*, pg. 263).

After the visit and seeing that the Monument was no longer of much interest to the public, I thought more about my letters and my experience. It was clear to me that, at the least, I wanted my children, both born years after the war was over, to learn about the war. It also seemed clear that simply assembling the letters and photographs would be confusing and, for my purposes, inadequate, and that if I did want my experience to be understood by my children, more effort was needed. I concluded if I wrote some remembrances, that those, along with the letters, photographs I had taken and drawings I had made, would form the basis for an interesting book.

There were already many books on Vietnam in print with more appearing daily. Many of those books, including some written by the generals and statesmen who developed the strategy as well as many by the grunts who carried the burden of the war on their weary backs, eloquently or passionately outlined very insightful views of the war. These books contained thoughtful analyses by very fine scholars on the war as well as heroic, harrowing and inspiring tales of the war. I wasn't sure whether additional words from me would add anything of significance to a body of literature that already seemed large and comprehensive.

But thinking about my children, I continued to feel that my personal story as a reluctant soldier would give them a more accurate perspective of me. The letters and photographs froze me in a time and place before I was married and before my children were born. With that in mind, I decided I would go ahead and write for my children and (perhaps) future grandchildren and if I told my story well, it might even be of interest to others..

For all its media coverage, and for all the television hours devoted to it, Vietnam, by and large, remained a personal, private experience for those who participated in it. When you went off to Vietnam, the rest of the country and the world were not at war; only you were at war. We arrived in Vietnam as individual replacements, not as part of a unit you had trained with. Then, we left Vietnam on our individual dates of departure and reentered the world as individuals - and rarely, if ever again, did we see many of the people we had been with in Vietnam and with whom we had a shared common set of experiences. Going and returning as individuals left us isolated as individuals, even as we participated in this most documented and public of American wars.

Not many of the men I went to college with went to Vietnam (I can't think of a single one.), but most of the men I grew up with in my small western New York State hometown did go. Some volunteered and some were drafted. However, Vietnam lasted so long and our service dates were strung out over so many years that it often seemed we served in different wars. We all had one war - but we each had our own personal private war story. I know one high school friend who served in MACV headquarters in Saigon early in the war, had a wonderful time and made a small fortune in blackmarket money transactions; but another served with the 1st Air Cavalry during a stretch of bitter fighting, and a third served with the 1st Infantry Division under the same circumstances. Later, after I returned, another was a forward air controller for the Air Force helping the ARVN troops after most US ground forces had left, and there were several who served in the Navy offshore. Each had a different view of Vietnam. Each had such a different experience. Additionally, for many, if not most draftees or enlistees who didn't stay in the Army, the war in Vietnam had no relationship to anything preceding the experience there and little or nothing to do with our subsequent lives. (I felt like some one had just snipped off a year of my life and put it aside.)

After I began writing, I was amazed at how much of the Vietnam experience was still vivid after all these years. As I kept writing it was also interesting how many things I discovered buried deeply in my mind. When I began consciously thinking about the past, at first it was as if I were seeing it through a distant telescope with flickering, disjointed images of memory. I began writing in a very tentative way, slowly constructing some order out of that jumble of images and half buried memories. But the more I began to write and look at the photographs, the more a strong current of memories that had been dammed up behind a wall of my other life after Vietnam began to flow. Events and emotions came rushing to the surface when I read words in the letters I had written so long ago. The same thing happened when I looked at the photographs. It is amazing to me how words and images have such evocative powers. The emotions they evoked were overwhelming, and sometimes the memories were so clear that it seemed that the place had just been visited or the event I remembered had happened only yesterday.

Other memories, of course, had been softened by the passage of time. While my recollections seem very clear, a lot has happened in those intervening years, and so I realize my memory may not be entirely historically accurate, for which I apologize.

It was during my work on the Memorial that I first began to try to understand my own Vietnam experience. That experience put me in touch with others who had a shared set of experiences and gave me, for the first time, a chance to talk at length with others around me who had similar feelings. It was at that time when I first encountered the Civil War letters of my great, great uncle Eugene Kingman. His letters, of which there are more than a hundred, along with selections from his diaries, were collected, edited and published in 1983 by my mother, Helene Kingman Phelan in a book titled *Tramping Out The Vintage*. Reading those letters led me to first examine his Army experience, but also to reflect on what happened to him after he was discharged. It is clear to me that the basic human emotions and the feelings of soldiers have not changed over time - loneliness, bravado, weariness, boredom, fear; all those emotions remain unchanged by the intervening years. Reading Eugene's letters helped me place the design concepts for the monument in a larger context, and so I talked about that with the other members of the Design Committee as the selection process for the memorial progressed. And, as it came to pass, it was the decision of the Committee that the New York City Vietnam Veterans' Memorial would incorporate quotes from letters home that vividly dramatized those often separate, but shared emotional journeys and similar experiences soldiers had in Vietnam.

So, those many years later, when my letters were returned to me and I began reading them, it was inevitable that I returned to my mother's book containing Eugene's letters. This time, those letters took on a different and much more immediate significance for me, and I began to think about incorporating them in this project.

Here was an ancestor who had also been involved in a great conflict and had left some letters documenting his experiences and feelings. Those letters resonated with me deeply and profoundly. Reading Eugene's words, I was often touched beyond belief.

For example, writing from Baton Rouge, Louisiana on February 13, 1863, to his beloved brother Charles 18 months after he had been in the Army :
"..While I am writing a terrible shower with heavy thunder and sharp lightening is raging outside our little tent, and inbetween the intervals between the flakes of fire it is pitchy dark all around excepting the long line of lights in the tents. I have been thinking tonight how long before this terrible war will come to an end, and I shall once more be able to pursue my studies and I have come to the conclusion that it will be a long while yet as things are managed...." (Tramping Out the Vintage, pg. 144)

I almost cried when I read those words, not just for Eugene, but because I remembered all those rainy nights when I sat in the hootch in Camp Eagle, writing letters under a naked light bulb, while I listened to the rain pounding down on the metal roof and had similar thoughts and dreams. And, I'm sure that all my hootch mates had the same thoughts. I'm also sure that all those who have been sent abroad to fight in a strange far - off place, whether it was Europe in World War I or II, Korea, or the Persian Gulf, have similar thoughts and write words like Eugene's.

So, my book is organized around my letters home combined with my photographs and drawings. It contains a side-bar of Eugene's story, mostly in his words. A mixture of documented facts (events recorded in the letters and photographs), frequently modified by commentary based on my memories of events, the book compresses time and space. As an artist, I recorded the visual memories in my photographs and drawings along with my letters, but in writing this I realized that the visuals and the words also evoked a powerful memory of the smells and sounds that were such a vivid part of the experience. I could not find a way to recreate those!

From my perspective, Vietnam divided the country like no war since the American Civil War and fundamentally changed the political landscape in America in ways that are still apparent today. For many people of my generation the divisions have still not completely healed. The America before Vietnam is very different from the America after Vietnam - just as America before the Civil War was dramatically different from the one that emerged from the ashes of that terrible conflict.

For readers the age of my children and younger, the Vietnam War seems to be an ancient war, viewed with a mixture of awe and fascination, yet detachment, overshadowed by current events such as the 1991 Gulf War, the September 11, 2001 attack on the World Trade Towers and our subsequent War on Terror including the invasion of Afganistan and Iraq. Yet, it seems to me that the Vietnam War, a very complex and complicated war in a complicated time, should continue to be of interest long after our current conflicts are concluded and I am gone. For those who read this story, I hope my modest account will contribute to a better understanding of the time and circumstances.

This manuscript has been privately printed in a very small edition and is intended as a personal memoir for an audience of children, family and friends.

Table of Contents

Preface 1

Chapter 1 13

Chapter 2 39

Chapter 3 67

Chapter 4 99

Chapter 5 129

Chapter 6 149

Chapter 7 185

Chapter 8 207

Chapter 9 215

Chapter 10 227

Acknowledgements 237

Bibliography 239

Chapter 1 - Prelude

For those of us growing up in the 50's or coming of age in the early 60's, the draft was a fact of life for young American males. And generally, since there had been relative peace since the cessation of the Korean conflict in the early 50's, the draft was neither feared or dreaded. The backdrop of the Cold War was ever present, but mostly it was a war of feints and bluffs, not of direct conflicts. So, if you had other career plans, the possibility of being drafted was little more than an annoyance. With a little luck you could avoid the draft since each draft board had relatively low quotas of draftees. By staying in college for an advanced degree you could probably avoid the unpleasantness

The author - c.1966

of being inducted. Since going to college was not the norm for young men (in the area) when I was graduated from high school, many of my high school classmates voluntarily entered the armed forces immediately after getting their diplomas. In 1969, eight years after my high school graduation, many of my high school classmates and friends had already volunteered or had been drafted, and a number had, by then, served in Vietnam. News of the war in the community was not just in the abstract. When veterans returned, they talked about their experiences, and news about those still serving there was shared in the community by their families. Everyone at home knew someone who was, or had been, in Vietnam. By then, the Draft had become a nightmare for many men and I faced making some difficult choices, as did many others.

I went off to college in 1961 and for the next few years gave the prospect of the Army only slight consideration. Only the Cuban Missile crisis caused a momentary concern. But by the late 60's, as the war in Vietnam heated up, the demands of the armed services for additional men increased, and the demands on the local draft boards were commensurately affected resulting in a change in the numbers and kinds of deferments granted. Additionally, each draft board was relatively autonomous, with each adopting specific strategies for meeting its quotas. Some granted deferments for selected professions deemed to be in the community interest. These professions generally demanded prior college training.

In 1969, hundreds of thousands of young Americans were receiving their draft notices since American involvement in Vietnam was then at its highest level, including more than 550, 000 soldiers, sailors, marines and airmen in Vietnam or on the seas nearby. As the war became less and less popular, college men of draft age became more sophisticated in finding ways to avoid the draft. Consequently most of the draftees were less well educated and tended to be 18 or 19 years old.

It was also a time when the debate over the war had become intertwined with other contentious social debates that were then causing great divisions in society - for example the debate over civil rights. Assassinations of men like John F. Kennedy, Robert Kennedy and Martin Luther King, along with the deadly urban riots taking place with increasing frequency in large U.S. cities, added to the already divisive social climate in the United States. Beginning in the summer of 1967 riots erupted in major US cities and continued every summer thereafter into the early 1970's.

Drafted

When I received my draft notice, on my 26th birthday in early May of 1969, I was teaching high school in my small home town named Almond in rural, Allegany County in Western New York State. Almond is located some 60 miles south of Rochester, not far from the Pennsylvania border. That is the beginning of the Allegany plateau which stretches south along the Eastern US, and it is a land of rolling hills and plateaus rising to about 2500 feet. Formed by retreating glaciers long ago, it was once a farming community, but by the 60's most of the farms were doing very poorly and many had already been abandoned with the resulting regeneration of the woodlands that had originally entirely covered the area.

I was not native to the area, having arrived at the age of 4 when my father took a job connected with the nearby university in Alfred. I spent my childhood and adolescence attending the small combined central school which served two communities and encompassed both primary and secondary schools where both my mother and father eventually taught. It was a tight-knit community. Even in the combined school the classes were small and so my graduating class numbered little more than 60 students. My childhood was spent happily doing all those things that small town children do. I played sports and also enjoyed the outdoors in activities such as camping, hunting and fishing. After graduating from high school, I went off to college in New York City, studying art and completing my undergraduate and masters degrees, all the while receiving student draft deferments.

A great deal of soul searching clarified my thoughts on the draft. Since I did not believe in killing another human for a cause that I did not believe in, I decided that while I would allow myself to be drafted and would serve, it would be as a conscientious objector. I had very strong views about what kind of personal behavior was appropriate for me in a cause that I could not support morally. If called, I would serve in the armed forces, but I did not want to be ordered to kill someone I had no quarrel with. I felt then, as I still do, that we were entering into an internal civil war that was tragic. I was also convinced that our direct participation would probably not make it any less so. Since I did not have a religious basis for this very firmly held conviction about being ordered to kill, I was destined for a difficult and contentious year of discussion with the Draft Board whose members were older men, most of whom were World War II veterans. They had a collective mind set that did not easily accept the validity of an individual with a conscience that would challenge national policy - no matter how flawed that policy might seem to the individual. With the Board in complete agreement with the then current Cold War ideology, American policy in Vietnam was seen as absolutely correct - and necessary.

In that era and in that place, anyone of draft age questioning national policy was seen as committing heresy, and so, while the Board would have been quite comfortable with my request to be classified as a conscientious objector on religious grounds, they were not at all comfortable with my request based on personal beliefs about the moral responsibility of individuals. Thus, after the Draft Board refused to grant me further deferments as a teacher, the board and I proceeded to go around and around for more than a year about my moral beliefs and my request for conscientious objector status. We had many appeals and many discussions, but after approximately 18 months, and after considering my last appeal, I was drafted into the Army, classified as a conscientious objector. In my case, out of consideration for my students, so the draft board said, my induction was deferred until July so I could finish the school year.

When I entered the Army, I was reluctantly convinced that I was doing my civic and patriotic duty even as I felt coerced. I was not a supporter of the Vietnam war, but I was an American, and in those days I believed in the concept of service. I think that John Kennedy's words "Ask not what your country can do for you, but what you can do for your country…" meant something to many of us then. I also had watched with considerable interest, and frequently with equal dismay, the lengths that some of my peers and contemporaries went to in order to receive deferments, to be classified 4-F, or even, in extreme cases, to dodge the draft by fleeing the country. After considering all these options and despite my reservations about the war, I ultimately concluded that I would not do those things.

Eugene Kingman

This column contains exerpts of letters and diary entries written by my great, great uncle Eugene Kingman. Born in 1844, the eldest son of Baptist Minister, Lebbeus Kingman and his wife Ruth, Eugene had six siblings, his beloved brother Charles and five sisters, Florance, Elizabeth (also known as Nancy), Adelaide (also known as Addie and later to be my great, great grandmother), Alice and Nellie.

Eugene was an eager volunteer, lying about his age and enlisting on October 12, 1861 with his best friend Mel Gould. Eugene thoroughly enjoyed his first few weeks in the Army, waiting while his regiment, the 12th Maine was brought up to full strength. This experience included his first train ride, and his letters home following his enlistment were all full of youthful enthusiasm. Writing to his family on November 17, 1861:

Dear Charley,

I received your letter that you write last when I was in Bangor. We are all well and prospering finally. Friday we were mustered into the service of the United States all the surimony [ceremony] we went through was to be examined and take the oath. We were examined all they did was ask us some few questions and if we answered to suit them we passed along. Today we are sitting around, some writing and some eating and some smoking and some reading their bible. My stock of money is about run out....
(Vintage pg. 12)

Writing to his mother a couple of days later, his hopes and grand ambitions for his Army service are voiced:

Dear Mother and Father and Brother and Sisters, the cat, the old cow, etc.

I will write today to tell you some news. I am well and have been ever since I left home. We are to receive

Inducted and in Training - July to November 1969

I experienced my first airplane journey from Buffalo to Philadelphia en route to Ft. Dix. But my mind was focused elsewhere and, as the subsequent letter indicates, I certainly lacked any enthusiasm for that as an adventure.

12 July
Dix
Hi

Just a note to let you know I'm alive and well
-happy NO
-unhappy NO
-Bored as hell
-crap upon more crap
-wasted time
- unbelievable.

We stayed in Buffalo for two days and didn't do a damn thing the first day. The second I filled out two forms.

Here more wasted time - by the way, the box which should arrive (courtesy of the Army) contains small stuff I can't use or keep - owing to the large quantity of Army crap I will have to take....

Five days later, I began my training at Ft. Sam Houston in San Antonio, Texas.

17 July
Hi,

Enclosed is my mailing address-

I haven't time to write now but I will say the Army

gets worse the further along I go (only 103 weeks to go!)

Really bad, no - even though I haven't started Basic and won't for a while (a week).

But bad - not as much what they are doing but what they are trying to do. Simply, it is conditioning (brainwashing!)

The sick product of our advanced (technologically) society!

Andy

20 July

I'm going to need a care package within a couple of weeks - a package of stamps and legal sized envelopes....

We won't start basic for another week and I wish it would start. I think once that's over a lot of the nonsense will let up...

Don't put any food in the package. We aren't supposed to have any goodies - bad for our stomachs while training. (The food is good here - much better than Dix - but not enough; even I who am not a big eater am constantly hungry!)....

News is brief and sketchy here - I know that (since this is Monday morning as I am finishing this up) that the astronauts are on the moon. But of course no access to a television or to magazines to see, what I'm sure, are spectacular sights.

The Army takes pains to keep us in isolation. The attempt (of course) is to make us forget there was ever any way of life except the Army way. (They don't call it brainwashing or any similarly nasty name - they call it indoctrination - but no matter the name, it is

our knap sacks and we are to be paid off tomorrow. I have signed the allotment roll for nine dollars a month which you will receive at home for the time I have served. I am going to be paid in full and I think that I shall buy a revolver for I am going to be an officer. A corporal it is true but I have done first rate in getting it for there are a good many men officers and good fellows that are privates. I am an officer now. Bully for me. ...I have done right I think so far and I try to do good. It is the general conviction that the war will not last more than six months longer. I am on the road to promotion. I like it so far for I think I have done right don't worry about me because I am doing as well as I can....
(Vintage, pgs 14 and 16)

From Dexter, he went first to Portland, Maine where he waited until the company was fully formed and then, traveling by boat and train, he continued his training at Camp Chase in Lowell, Massachusetts.

I read with great amusement the expressions of his youthful idealism, since I had none of that.

Eugene was entranced with the aspects of the Army that I disliked the most:: the parades and the endless drill. Writing his father on December 8:

"We are all contented and we are as happy as could be expected and I never was healthier in my life. Today we have had a grand review and inspection by General Butler and I would have given $5.00 if you and the rest had been here to see us go through the inspection... " (Vintage, pg. 22)

His unflagging enthusiasm for the adventurous life he was experiencing - even if it was mixed in with a touch of homesickness at times - is clear in his subsequent letters containing very detailed descriptions of the camps he stayed in and his training. In a long letter, written from Camp Chase on December 22, 1861 to his mother he says in relation to one of his companions who was released:

...Al Abbot has been discharged because he is sick and I fear he has got the consumption.... He was not able to stand the hardships we have to go through; although I have and never was better in my life and so has Mell

brainwashing!)

And believe me, it seems that I have been in the Army much longer than two weeks.

Give my love to Grandmother!

I arrived for my training in the full blast furnace heat of the south Texas summer and so I spent the summer and early fall months doing all the physical activities that the Army basic training requires. In point of fact, the heat of the summer in San Antonio turned out to be great mental and physical conditioning for the heat I would encounter in Vietnam. However, while I was in Texas I did not appreciate the heat or those endlessly clear and hot summer days filled with the seemingly endless, strenuous physical activity that often started in the hour before dawn and lasted until early evening.

I began to try to find a way to use my art training. In an undated letter to my parents (in an envelope postmarked 30 July, 1969):

Hi,

Another request - which I would like shortly (as soon as possible!) Some slides of my work - about 30. (In my room there are two trays of slides.) I would like the slides to be distributed among my work - some drawings (blue pencil) of the figure, some of my realistic paintings (such as the portrait of Betsy) some of the older stylized work and one or two of my latest stuff! Please pick the best possible & a fairly wide variety but those that show technical knowledge.

I'm going to try and get an appointment with personnel which I missed today because I had minor surgery - a mole removed from the top of my mouth. When they were compiling my dental record it was noticed and the recommendation was that it come out. Not that there was anything wrong - it just happened to be in an unusual place. (By the way, I haven't smoked in almost a week!)

Magazines were very nice to get! Would appreciate some more in a couple of weeks. Stamps came today!

Finally started Basic yesterday & will be finished in 6 weeks.

When I get my slides I'll try to see Special Services to find out if I might work something out there if this other thing doesn't work out! (The other would be a job of some sort within the medical corps.)

Surprisingly - getting mail is depressing. I'm eager to get it but then feel badly afterwards. (Prison mentality!)

In the future don't send any bank statements unless I ask you to. Just put them in a pile.

My best to everyone!
Andy

Gould. We have had as hard times as we shall likely to see, although you may not believe it and yet I like [it] first rate for I made up my mind for a hard time.... (Vintage, pg 29)

Of course, he had not experienced as hard times as he was destined to discover.

He also writes of his intention to keep a diary:

...I am going to commence the first of next year, if I live, to write in my diary and keep my accounts straight. Perhaps you would like to know the circumstances under which I write. I am writing on a gun box set up to the fire and resting on my knees before it for light. I have a small bit of a candle and some fire light. There are eight of the boys in here making all the noise they can and the noise outside is like thunder only a great deal more discordant, it is good discipline for me to collect my thoughts amid the noise....(Vintage pgs 29 and 30)

That promise he kept, and for the remainder of his term of enlistment he wrote home regularly, often in great detail, and frequently illustrated the letters with drawings and diagrams. He also kept a

21

dairy. It was very interesting to me that he asked his family to keep all his letters, "for I want these safe for when I get home." (Vintage, pg. 34) It was also very interesting that one of the reoccuring themes in his letters is his need to get funds from home to supplement Army rations, and these requests began very soon after he joined. Later requests for money continued, but he asked for the funds for stamps, paper, clothing and shoes. Paper and stamps were expensive, and items of clothing were necessary, as worn clothing was not quickly replaced by the Army.

When I began comparing Eugene's letters to mine, I began to reflect on my experiences and attitudes wondering why I was so negative. Of course I had been drafted, and I was older. These were the obvious answers, but a more basic answer lay in the fact that, along with his youthful innocence and enthusiasm for what he saw as an adventure, Eugene had a very strong moral conviction that he had done the right thing. He was convinced that fighting for the Union was both right and absolutely necessary.

On the other hand, it also seemed to

Writing to my sister and her husband few weeks later:

Aug 10

Texas

Betsy & Steve,

Thanks for the letter - things sound like they are going well for you.

Have a couple of requests to make! First - what happened with the lens I left with you to be repaired?? Did Sean pay for it? Second - if you still have the list of people to write to (in the Army) in the Visual aids or Graphics Dept - send them on! I've applied for a Special Services position (have to phone tomorrow or the next - but the application is in!) If that doesn't work out I'll try the post Illustrator, etc. Just see if I have anything to peddle & whether there are any buyers here. What the hell, nothing to lose! (Except the whole state of Texas and the entire 4th Army which they could drop in the Gulf of Mexico for all I care!) Anyway, anything to ease my stay.

Have had two weeks of basic now & while the physical exercise is considerable, the hardest thing (as Sassi warned me !) is staying awake in class! Yes, we have classes - field sanitation, guard duty & other such academic toughies!

The Army really sucks! In many ways I'm sorry I didn't have the moral courage to go to jail. That though, is relative. (But the Army still sucks! That's all I have to say at the moment!)

Andy

P.S. By the way - I got a very nice note from Judy wishing me luck.

Another letter to Betsy and Steve followed two weeks later:

>Aug 24
>
>Texas
>
>Betsy & Steve,
>
>Enjoyed the magazines - the pictures look great! Very glad to hear things are going so well.
>
>Got a letter from Susie Platt the other day - she's in NYC now, working at NYU as a receptionist. She said she had thought about calling you but thought you probably were still mad about that weekend in Feb (when she never showed up!). I told her to go ahead and call you - that I doubted you held grudges that long! She sounded very lonely. (She is living with a girlfriend but apparently she is hard to take!) Anyway - you may get a call from her.
>
>Glad to hear you're having the lens fixed & that its going on your bill. ...I haven't received any pay yet so you may have to carry the lens for a few weeks! (Now that you are affluent-!)
>
>Not only did I get a letter from Judy (surprise) but also from Susanjean! She sounds very happy - which is just great. Says she is trying to get you two up to Marblehead.
>
>I'm headed up into the hills this coming week for bivouac. More shit (almost the last except for tests the next week). Last week the big event was the gas chamber! Have gotten the hang of getting out of the Company area on weekends - spent yesterday (and now am spending today) in a distant P.X. Cafeteria. Last night I went to a baseball game (desperation - anything to break the routine!) hoping to get away but found it was tightly supervised. (The Army believes in

me that he was yearning for adventure and seeking a way to document his passage to manhood. I saw many like Eugene when I was in the Army. Even then, for all the discussions about the rightness or wrongness of war in Vietnam, there were still many young men who believed as passionately about the rightness of our involvement in Vietnam as did Eugene about the duty of the North to preserve the Union.

Unlike me, after finishing training Eugene went, with no home leave, directly from Camp Chase to Boston where he boarded the Ship Constitution (not the famous one) enroute for his duty station. He wasn't sure where it would be, but he should have been since Butler raised his regiments for an express purpose - the Louisiana Campaign.

Dear Brother,

>*I have not had a chance to write you before since I came aboard*

taking care of its own!) Sometimes I believe there is a proscribed manner for wiping your ass (AR 36824 - 3 probably!) There seems to be a regulation for every situation.

Speaking of situations - I'll be finishing up here on the 5th of Sept. Whether or not my permanent party status comes through by then remains to be seen. I do know that I have been requested as a permanent party (as a clerk) to be detailed to the Training Aids as an Illustrator. Chances are pretty good that I won't even be trained as a Medic, but will end up with an MOS (Method of Service) of a clerk (and later Illustrator). If I don't receive medical training that would probably (given the clerks MOS) mean an office job at the worst and an Illustrator's at best! Far better than jacking my ass around in the Infantry as a Medic!

Yesterday (morning) I had to march in a parade (which of course was dull, hot and dusty!) but where else could you have a parade with about 2000 men and have only 2 rifles present! Only at a Med Training Center!!

By the way - Happy Anniversary! (I must write to Dad to say happy Birthday also!)

Will let you know what the hell is happening as soon as I know.

Andy"

From this vantage point, thirty years later, it is both fascinating and sad for me to read this and to see how I was trying so desperately to find a way to be assigned to a position that would allow me to use my training as an artist - and also hopefully - to keep me from being sent to Vietnam.

24

And, the letter to my parents of the same day:

Aug 24
Texas

Hi,

Just a note to say Happy Birthday to Dad!

Slides finally got here./ Am going to send most of them back (toward the end of the week!)

Nothing new to report on what I will be doing except that I know that I have been requested as Permanent party (as a clerk).

Thanks for the money - I hope I get paid this Friday! (I think I will.)

If so will probably send some on to you to deposit (or hold) for me - am not quite sure how I can do some things. I think you could deposit cash in my Alfred Account - my New York account will be a bit more difficult. Will face that problem when I do actually get paid!

This week bivouac, next week final tests & that's all of Basic. (Thank God!)

Thanks for the Camera 35 (magazine) but don't send any others! Some are worth keeping (reference) which I can't do here!

News of Bob Torrey [a high school teacher and friend who died of a heart attack] *a real shock. I wrote Audrey a note.*

Got copies of New York Mag with Steve's pictures (and a letter) from Betsy! Looks good.

My best,
Andy

and I had no chance at all now. You have probably read in the Journal how we passed through Boston and embarked. That will tell you the story better than I could. How long we shall stay here I don't know nor does anyone else. We may stay here a week or longer and we may sail tonight. I hope we shall....

....I suppose that we are to leave today and I cannot write but a line or two. I do not think we shall go to Ship Island but to Point Royal or some other place....(Vintage, pgs 37 and 39)

On January 21, 1862 from Old Point Comfort, near Fort Monroe, he writes :

"*....I hope that the war will [get]close soon for I am impatient to see it and we all want to meet the rebels and have a fight but I don't want government to shove us around in old ships and rot we have been aboard 18 days and we all hate it....*"
(Vintage, pg 42)

This was the first (but not the last) time he railed against the government.

25

I suffered through the mind-numbing and sometimes (in my opinion) senseless parts of our training - the classes, the long marches, calisthenics, and the endless close order drill. But physically, I toughened up and also mentally made the transition, learning in small ways how to make the most of the situation and the mentality. For example, once, when on KP duty, I was assigned to clean out a refrigerator. I quickly discovered that there were worse assignments possible in the kitchen and so I spent all afternoon cleaning that refrigerator, much to the disgust of the Sergeant, who wanted to assign me to other duties but who, finding me working away diligently every time he came by, couldn't appear to be contradicting his own orders by taking me off the job before it was complete. I just kept working away, letting my mind drift in a daze while scraping off crud - very slowly. (As a digression, it is interesting to note that I went from being a teacher of 18 year olds to being their peer in basic training about two weeks later. It was quite an interesting experience, and, in order to escape the latent resentments and prejudices of drill instructors, I quickly learned to avoid any acknowledgment of my college degrees and teaching experience.)

Before I was drafted, my Grandmother, then in her mid 80's, had come up to Almond, to live near my parents, and had given me permission to build a darkroom in her basement. So, during the two years I lived in Almond while I was teaching and battling with the Draft Board, I spent a great deal of time at her house and, of course, spent time talking with her about the war and my situation. She was my only living grandparent, and, as I was her oldest grandchild and had often visited her during summers as a youngster, we already had a very close relationship which only grew closer during those two years prior to my service when I saw so much of her. This shows in my letters to her, never more so than in a letter to her written after almost two months in the Army. I felt very comfortable in writing an angry letter, expressing many of my feelings about the Army to her in a rather blunt way:

Aug 29
Texas

Dear Grandmother,

I'm sorry I haven't written sooner but there really hasn't been much to say about the Army. There still isn't - I dislike it even more than before and probably will increasingly continue to do so. The Army is for adolescents, for men that still like to play with toys that go "bang"! If one enjoys playing those games then one can enjoy the Army. Unfortunately, I stopped playing those games a few years ago!

We were out on Bivouac last week (a hike, camp-out simulated field conditions) and while we were marching we would be attacked with tear gas, smoke grenades, etc. by a young Lt. He was playing a game - the way he (and another Lt) were cavorting around reminded me of a couple of 10 yr olds playing "hide & seek" or "Cowboys & Indians". This to them, was a game. So is the real thing (war) I'm sure!

It rained every day while on Bivouac so that made life unpleasant also.

Sean tells me you paid for a new tailpipe for the station wagon for which I would like to thank you!

Back to more negative comments about the Army. I am really more and more horrified by the amount of money being spent and how war & the upkeep of

Armies is so damned expensive - even the training of Armies is incredible. It is just a crime that the money spent on destruction so out weighs the amount spent on constructive things. I don't give a damn how much or how many benefits are derived from military research, etc. If the money was re-applied in the beginning we would have so much more.

That's enough of that - but I really am horrified by it. My sense of dislike, distrust and dismay of the military mind has increased greatly.

Clearly, I was sick of basic training and Army. Also, it seems that the seemingly endless San Antonio summer heat had me on edge, and so, after venting my anger and frustration some more, I finished the letter this way:

I hope everything is well with you. Fall must be starting to color the foliage slightly by now. Something I have discovered is how much I enjoy the climate of Upstate N.Y. - including the snow! I don't enjoy 104 degree temperatures.

We went out to Camp Bullis for our field exercises that would last for several days. We would camp there for several nights. I still have vivid memories of the exercises in night orientation with escape and evasion maneuvers when we would be driven to a distant point and then have to navigate back to our camps which were guarded. We were required to try to infiltrate back into our camp - where, if we were successful, a hot meal and some time to rest awaited us. Inevitably, I would run headlong into the Texas sized spider webs that were spun between trees. Many of them were so strong you sometimes literally bounced off them instead of breaking through them - or you got tangled in them and spent a frantic few minutes getting out of them while you worried if the spiders were going to try to wrap you up for dinner. I don't think I was ever really terrified of the spiders, just amazed that they were that big and the webs they spun were that strong.

Advanced Medical Training

In a letter to my parents, undated but the envelope has a September 14, 1969 postmark, I requested some civilian clothing to be sent to me, since with the completion of Basic Training, I would have the opportunity to get passes and leave Ft. Sam Houston on some weekends. I also wrote the following :

> *...My hair actually changes direction when I run a comb through it (at least on top). Not that it is long - While AIT* (Here I really meant - advanced medical training) *is not really hard so far it is busy - we've had about 10 hrs instruction in bed making this week (along with various other subjects Anatomy & Physiology, etc - and some completely irrelevant such as Character Guidance.)*
> *Not that I am really enjoying it....*

Then I wrote to my sister and her husband:

Sept. 14
Betsy & Steve,

> *First, my address except for the third line is the same - third line should now read Co D, 3 Bn, Class 64 - also I am now Pvt E-2! (I fucked up and scored too*

high on my combat proficiency test and much to my disgust was high man in my class - they even gave me a plaque for that!) Will return to that later!

Also was fucked up in the Illustration job - I am now at AIT (here I again meant AMT) *training to be a Medical Corpsman! Ten hours of bed making already (believe it or not I think we have another ten hours!) and this is only the first week. By now my mood is one of acceptance, (although it is reluctant and guarded) but earlier in the week I was really pissed off. The illustration still may come off after AIT - the Cpt has re-applied for me. Anyway - I didn't want to (and don't want to) become a medic. Worse still is the fact that I have landed in a gung-ho company. Mother of Christ - we have a marching inspection every fucking morning! We march to and from every class with drums beating and flags flying! No kidding - we had a lot of spit and polish in Basic - but more here. And of course it makes less sense than ever - I mean the company, the MTC, the Army, the war, etc.*

For example - I find the army just filled up with absurdities and contradictions - but we are continually exhorted about defending freedom! Yet last Sunday we were all prevented from attending Church (or saying we were attending church when really we went to the cafeteria) - that's right, last Sunday we were told we couldn't leave the barracks. Yet this Sunday (today) we were forced to go to Church - damn right, all 550 men were marched in formation up to the church door. Protestants one church; Catholics another - we weren't forced in but we were damn well marched right up to the door. I guess freedom is having a choice of which formation you wished to march in! Believe it or not this... barracks I am in is mainly CO's [conscientious objectors] - we all came over from Basic together and so essentially we have the same group who went through basic together (along with a few new ones). It is turning out to be a sharp class - I don't believe these people but they (CO's) can actually be as gung-ho (or more so) than others!....anyway this damned group of CO's have turned out to be gung-ho and they are pushing hard for Honor Company. Starched fatigues every other day - boots like patent leather every day. Marching like machines (I have to admit that even I have learned to march well!) Anyway there is a lot of shit that the Army loves to have polished (and if you've ever tried to polish faeces [feces] you know how hard it is!) Really this is a spit and polish place - must be quite impressive to one who enjoys military parades to watch 1000 people converge in tight formations with drums beating and feet stamping in those measured military rhythms. (What a fantastic waste of energy!)

Truly; the Army dissipates more constructive energy than any other institution we have....

Have been throwing the words down on paper just to get something down. Will try to be more careful in how I say things - I am torn by trying to get everything down on paper (and hoping it makes sense to others) but not wanting to have something get confused. Not that extreme clarity of expression is the goal (why the hell attempt that when you are writing letters as a soldier and when all you wish to convey is the mood of the situation; to transfer some of your trauma to another; to dissipate some of your despair and anger. To convey the feeling of futility at fighting an institution which doesn't even allow you the privilege of acknowledging your existence as a person

- only as a number!.....hell, look at the Army - for years they have been fighting off that dreaded implacable enemy called "the people's desire for Peace." Otherwise known as "Ban the Bomb", "make love not War" and other similarly seditious slogans all emanating from the outsiders - civilians. So to protect the loyal soldier he is bombarded with cleansing slogans and (forced into) habits designed to nullify the normal impulse to slovenly lassitude and peace. (To be able to sleep past 6 AM on Sunday would be a small piece of heaven!)

 Anyway - back to a mood of conventionality. I am discouraged and getting more disgusted every day. Yesterday I got into civilian clothes for the first time since July and spent the afternoon in the PX Cafeteria (still not allowed off base) and then I went to a movie last night at the post movie theatre. (Movie - The Prime of Miss Jean Brodie) Which was not a good movie. Anyhow everything I did simply increased my feeling of isolation. The movie became irrelevant because it happened "out there" and in the Army one has no need to concern one's self with that.

 Anything I've said in this letter is not new - you have heard it from me before. (And probably will hear it again!) I'm sure it is simply a desperate attempt to find (acceptable) reasons to why insanity exists (and why I can't live in harmony with it!) So - pardon the lack of coherence but I did need to write a letter like this - to serve as a catharsis at the least!

 I hope the Rep is turning out well. Have you found an apt/studio yet? Looking? I'm sure you're making money (even if uncollected as yet)!

Andy

Never did explain that Basic Training Score! Some time!

This is the one letter that survives in which I just let my bitterness, anger and frustration pour out on the pages. (Later, other letters like this were sent to some of my friends from Vietnam when I was in an equally black mood there, but as far as I know they have all been lost.)

After the incident described in my letter of September 14, we still were usually granted permission to attend Sunday services and so continued conducting our own services at a base PX coffee shop with the Sunday paper as our scripture. It was truly a time of spiritual rejuvenation.

In the context of this whole experience, where, I tried, in vain, to get an alternative assignment as an army illustrator, it became clear to me how lucky I had been in my previous existence where I had been able to choose what I did with my life. I was devastated by the thought that I would be mindlessly assigned by the Army to do a task for which I had no aptitude nor prior training, and I just couldn't understand (in my naivete) the reason or reasons that it could or would happen that way. As a civilian, I was able to contribute to society in a way that I felt suited my talents, but I was now in the Army, and, contrary to civilian life, the Army determined your fate by their immediate needs - regardless of your prior training. All this gave me insight into the despair that people must feel if they happen to be born and grow up in societies with planned economies where the freedom to plan one's life and choose one's own professional career is denied. In the value system of the US Army in 1969, with a war going on in Vietnam, medics were far more important than illustrators. There was a war going on, casualties were high and medics were in great demand. The Army couldn't train medics (and infantry soldiers) fast enough to meet the needs in Vietnam.

Many (but not all) of the other men training as medics were doing so because they had requested it for moral or religious reasons. There were, for example, a number of men who were Seventh Day Adventists, as well as Friends (Quakers), and other conscientious objectors with their own personal objections to killing. They all were a very interesting and, in many ways, an unlikely group of soldiers. In our conversations it was clear that, while no one was willing to be an active participant in taking another's life, all of us had a sense of duty and responsibility that allowed us to face the prospect of being sent into combat without bearing arms. Everyone embraced strong moral convictions and values, and, whether or not they were based on religion, all the soldiers there (including me) were demonstrating a willingness to entertain the very strong possibility that they could (and most would) be sent into a situation as Army Medics that included service under very hostile conditions - namely Vietnam. We believed, for various reasons that we would try to serve our country while preserving our own moral, religious or spiritual sense of what was right or wrong.

Much of the medical training was quite rudimentary, but some of it was very interesting after you got used to the routine of the army. Some of it - for example the parts about training for duty as a medical orderly - were just boring and awful. They included such things as how to change the bedpan of invalid patients or how to change sheets with patients still in the bed. On the other hand, learning how to haul stretchers across an obstacle course under live ammo fire was fascinating in a macho way. Also interesting was learning how to carry one of your classmates under the various and none-too -favorable conditions of combat. Much of the training was designed to have you learn the basics of trauma control and casualty evacuation - getting the wounded out of the field of fire, then stopping their bleeding and stabilizing them while awaiting evacuation to a field hospital where well trained medical personnel with sophisticated facilities would perform the real medical procedures. As a result, I received a superficial introduction to some aspects of medical matters during the training. By and large the real basics of medicine and pharmacology that I later employed in Vietnam, were learned on the job - where I needed to know them.

San Antonio and the Texas Hill Country

During the months when I was at Ft. Sam Houston, I got a few chances to explore San Antonio and the nearby Hill Country of Texas. While these events weren't very frequent, I did get a day or a weekend off (or part of one) on a few occasions. When that happened, I enjoyed sampling a few of the pleasures of the city of San Antonio, which is a city I found charming. In those very busy and physically tiring days, simple pleasures were really something that I appreciated.

In downtown San Antonio, the River Walk was within a comfortable distance from our barracks on Ft. Sam Houston, and once discovered, the Walk became a treasured cool, quiet refuge for those few Sunday afternoons that I managed to finesse into a few hours off base. It wasn't as popular then as it is now and consequently was much more relaxed. We found a number of restaurants where you could linger over a plate of enchiladas and a couple of Carta Blancas for several hours while watching the boats go by on the canal or reading the Sunday paper. Also located very close to Ft. Sam Houston was the Alamo, and I became fascinated by it and the huge role that small piece of real estate played in the history of Texas. The grounds of the Alamo were shady and cool and even quiet on many days (in contrast to its violent history) and so, like the Riverwalk, the Alamo was a place where I would go and read for a few precious hours as an escape from life in the Army.

I discovered, almost by accident one day, another of San Antonio's delights: the McNay Art Museum, which, much to my surprise and wonderment, held a treasure trove of some of Paul Klee's works. Those infrequent, but treasured, weekend passes allowed for a trip to Austin and one to the Texas Hill Country. The passes, which were a time of real discovery for me since I had never been to Texas prior to this, included a visit one weekend to the ranch home of one of my basic training friends in nearby Weimar, Texas. The ranch was small by Texas standards, but so serene and beautiful it hardly seemed possible that such an oasis could exist so close to the bustle of San Antonio, where Ft. Sam Houston, along with Lackland/ Kelly and Brooks Air Force Bases were located. Our host, Jim also drove us around the hill country and we saw the countryside and some of the little towns (settled largely by German immigrants) including many that were laid out around a town square, all of which were very interesting and reminded me of New England towns.

But by the end of October, our training was winding down, and we were all nervously awaiting our orders - which we all expected would send us to Vietnam. Individually we each hoped we would be one of the rare exceptions who was assigned stateside or sent overseas but not to the combat zone. We went through RVN training, and all the sergeants told

us that we would be heading for Nam. Upon completion of my advanced training, my MOS (Military Operational Specialty) was 91A10 - or, simply put, I was a Medic. (Later, after being promoted to PFC, I would become a 91B20.) Since the war in Vietnam was roaring along at historically high levels of American combat involvement, it was clear that most of the medics being trained were going to be needed in combat units.
I wrote my parents:
"Nov 2

> *Enclosed is a list of things I'd like sent to Betsy & Steve's to meet me. I'm still assuming I'll get in N.Y.C. the evening of the 14th.*
> *We go out to Camp Bullis for a 3 day practical exercise this week and then I have a final week of RVN (Republic of Viet Nam) Training - actually only a couple of days! Plus administrative chores.*
> *It looks like I will store most of my Army equipment & will get a new issue for Vietnam. However it is, I'll get instructions - in fact probably an abundance of them.*
> *I really don't know exactly what I'll do with whatever time I have.*
> *Also enclosed is my insurance policy - which I will pay when I get some money transferred into my checking account! I don't like keeping it here as things will be too hectic."*

For most of us the inevitable happened: on the 10th of November we received orders reassigning us to the US Army Overseas Replacement Station Oakland California, (ultimate assignment VN Trans Det [WQBR] APO SF 96384) with a reporting date of 3 December, 1969 with 16 days delay enroute authorized.

Weimar, Texas (from my sketchbook)

Chapter 2
To 'Nam and then North to I Corps

A brief leave

During my 16 day leave, I spent Thanksgiving with my family in Almond before shipping out to Vietnam. It was a bittersweet time, and it turned out to be the last time I saw my Grandmother Coogan. A very strong woman, with a distinctive personality and character that had enabled her to raise five children after her husband died, she was not much given to sentimentality. But she cried disconsolately when I left, telling me that she had seen her father, husband, son and now her grandson go off (or prepare to go off) to wars. She said it was too much and that she had seen and heard about too many wars for any one person to bear. Mentioning her uncle Eugene Kingman (the first time I heard his name) and her memories of him after his return from the Civil War, she also spoke of her preparations to take her own young children to live with her parents when it appeared certain that her husband was to be

A page from my note book

drafted in WW I. Four years of anxiety about her son Richard and son-in-law Bruner Hardy (who had married her youngest, my Aunt Isobel) when they went off to World War II, had drained her. I believe she knew she would never see me again.

From Almond, I went to NYC spending a few days with Betsy and Steve and seeing a variety of friends before flying out to Oakland, California on the first of December, 1969 for processing prior to my departure to Vietnam. That time in NYC was very strange; all my friends and others with whom I came in contact were talking about their plans for the future, whereas I was wondering if I had a future beyond the next few weeks. Bound into a system and no longer free to choose my own course, whatever happened to me in the coming months would be my destiny and I knew that was beyond my control. Whatever my fate, I had to accept it and make the best of whatever situation I found myself in. It was a strange position for me to be in and led to some strange conversations when someone, after expounding on his or her own plans, would then innocently ask me what I would be doing in the near future. I tried to answer, but usually couldn't. I was in awe of people confidently proceeding with plans for their lives while I was completely unable to anticipate anything except that I had to report to the US Army Overseas Replacement Station in Oakland on December 3, 1969, "not earlier than 0800 hours and not later than 1200 hours on date specified for overseas movement."

When I arrived in Oakland, most of the guys who had been in training with me were either already there or arrived shortly thereafter. It was a bittersweet reunion of sorts while we waited for our processing and our flights.

There were a few men who never showed up - they went AWOL. They went for many reasons, and what happened to most of them I never really knew, but I heard rumors about several. I did know directly about one man, who had become a friend in both basic and advanced training. He had dropped hints that he wasn't going to show up in Oakland. After he didn't show, I learned about him from others whom he had called while on leave saying he was going AWOL and was headed to Canada; but then later when I was in Vietnam (and after) I got letters directly from him.

When I was in Vietnam, I got a letter from him explaining why he had gone AWOL: he was terrified of going into war, he simply hadn't been able to face it. He apologized to those of us who had been his friends and who had gone to Nam. He expressed not only his guilt, but the anguish he felt. He first fled to Canada and then, when that country no longer offered a legal haven for those refusing the draft or deserting from the armed forces on moral grounds, he eventually went on to Sweden which had begun granting asylum to US draft dodgers and to those US armed forces deserters who could prove that they were deserting based on a refusal to serve in Vietnam. After I returned to the States he kept in touch and wrote letters telling me about his life in terms that frequently seemed homesick and wistful. After a few years the letters became increasingly infrequent as he began to come to terms with his exile. Then, for the next several years, I would get a note or a card about once a year from him. When I last heard from him, he had married a Swedish girl and seemed to be permanently settled in Stockholm. Then the letters stopped - and whether he returned to the United States after the general amnesty President Carter signed in the late seventies, or whether he stayed on in Sweden, I don't know. But there were others like him, members of my generation who left the country to avoid the draft or, if drafted, deserted to avoid serving in the war. As a result, before the war and the draft ended in the early 70's,

Eugene Goes to War

Eugene was a far better letter writer than I was, constantly writing to his parents, his brother or his sisters, keeping them up to date on his various activities.

I read with both amusement and amazement about Eugene's eagerness to go off to war; since in those days getting there took some time. The business of war was still a game to him and the reality of it was inconceivable since the last war was buried in the distance past. There was no television to remind him of the dire consequences. In a letter dated January, 1862, and marked Fort Monroe, which lay at the head of the Chesapeake Bay in sight of the Confederate lines, he wrote:

Dear Mother,

Here we are away down south in Dixie and it is real pleasant. We have not yet gone ashore but I think we shall. It hardly seems as though we are truely in sight of rebel ground, but so it is. We are lying close to the fort and in full sight of the rip raps and Levels Point, Virginia, and the rebel buttresses. We left Boston Monday and expected to arrive here in 48 hours sail

there was a sizable contingent in Sweden of young American males avoiding service in the US Army.

The Oakland Army facility was a big holding pen and was the primary facility processing soldiers for the Vietnam war machine. I remember it as a series of big hanger-like buildings where we got fed and slept, awaited orders, and where we were issued some of our Vietnam clothing. While the Army bureaucracy worked at what seemed to be a snaillike pace, we were eventually sorted and processed and put on flights to Vietnam. In reality it didn't take very long. I arrived in Oakland on the 1st of December and by December 6 I was in Vietnam, but it seemed like an eternity. There was not much for us to do. We pulled some KP duty, but otherwise we were simply confined, and so, since we all worried about the future, we talked endlessly and aimlessly. I had taken some books with me, but frequently I was too nervous and preoccupied to concentrate on anything except the most escapist kind of reading. My notebook reads: "Waiting for the plane - the last hour spent doing that most American of all things - watching T. V." Looking back at my orders, issued in common with others as a list, I can see that there were a lot of 91A10's with me on that flight!

One World to Another

One hundred and eight years after Eugene went to war, complaining about spending days on ships or by rail, we flew to Vietnam in about 16 hours on commercially chartered flights complete with "coffee, tea or me" stewardesses - who were cute, dressed in trim uniforms complete with short skirts. (As I recall, they were well trained to deflect the often crude and very direct advances of a planeload of GI's going off to war.) The irony of it was not lost on me... I wrote cryptically in my notebook: *"A very strange way to go to war with pretty stewardesses and all the comforts of a civilian flight...."* While the flight from Oakland to Saigon (Ton Son Nut) only took 16 hours, we lost a day on the flight - which if we survived, we would get back upon our return.

We stopped for refueling and had a chance to stretch our legs in Hawaii in the middle of the night, then flew over the Philippines in the early morning and swept into the Bien Hoa airport in the heat of the afternoon. (*"Red-brown sandy looking soil as we cross the coast of Vietnam,"* I wrote.) As we deplaned and walked across the white hot tarmac, sweating and huffing under the weight of our duffle bags and in the full glare of the tropical sun, we were greeted with a great cheer by a waiting group of ragtag soldiers in worn, faded, mud and sweat stained jungle fatigues. I was puzzled at first, and then I suddenly realized why they were cheering. They were doing so because it was our plane that would carry them "back to the world", a phrase I would soon come to know well, but whose ironic meaning was lost on me at the moment. My passage was swift. Yesterday I had been in The World, but now I was not. Now, I was in Vietnam.

From the airport we went by bus to Long Binh, the huge Army in-country processing center (near the US Air Force's Ton Son Nut airbase) where we were housed for about 3 days - if memory serves me correctly - while we were processed prior to receiving our Vietnam assignments as replacements to the various units. The Army did not assign whole units to Vietnam after the initial dispatch of an entire Division or Brigade, but sent over individuals as replacements for personnel already there who had completed their "tour of duty" or, on a rotating basis, to replace casualties. The normal tour of duty for a soldier was one year. (The date you completed your tour of

but the weather came up thick and foggy and we could not make in until yeaterday about noon. I was not seasick hardly any on the whole voyge though we had some rather rough weather... (Vintage pg. 39)

Ft. Monroe, was supposed to be a short layover. But while Ft. Monroe was only a lay-over, it was long and it wasn't until February 5, that the ship assigned to take him south headed out to sea.

Writing his sister Alice on February 5, 1862, while still on the Constitution, his letter refers to the intricate web of family and friends in small towns at that time:
Dear Sister Alice,

I write this letter to you for a birthday present for it is all that I can give you. We came aboard the ship last Sunday while you were all at meeting I suppose...

Yesterday just as we were going to sail and it was the last chance I got a letter from home with yours and Charley's pictures and a dollar bill in it, but the letter was worth to me 5 dollars and the pictures 5 more for I had not got one before for over a month and I was very anxious to hear from home. I think of you verry verry often and wish I could see you but I

Another page from the notebook

must wait and help Uncle Sam a little first for he needs me more than I am needed at home. I hope to see him out of his trouble by another winter so I can go through college and be something although I am of some use now I hope....

Tell Aunt Betsy that I will write her next time and tell all the rest that I will to them in their turns. Mel Gould has got all well now and is round with us. when we were on shore we lived first rate we had rice and fresh beef and hominy and syrup and beans,etc., etc.and we cooked it ourselves in our tents so we had just what we wanted....There now I think that I have written you a good long letter and tell the rest to write me....
(Vintage, pgs 45 and 46)

Eugene Kingman chose to enlist in the Army, for reasons it seemed to me, that related to finding a purpose and a cause he could support. I believe he discovered himself while in the Army. As part of that process, and very early in his enlistment, he discovered his talent for drawing. Even more importantly, he also discovered that his talent was

duty was known as your DEROS date. It became an obsession for most soldiers.)

Among other things our in-country processing in Long Binh included being outfitted with additional gear to supplement the new uniforms we had received in Oakland. Some of the items included a poncho and a poncho liner as well as olive drab underwear and other miscellaneous "stuff" - canteens, pistol belts, etc. Our uniforms, previously issued in Oakland, consisted of tropical weight nylon BDU's (fatigues) along with two pairs of jungle boots. We were coaxed to give up our field jackets, as unnecessary in the tropical climate, a decision I reluctantly acquiesced in, and would very shortly regret. We also turned in our standard weight stateside fatigues as well. We were assured by the harried clerks that helmets, flak jackets and other items would be issued when we got to our units.

No one I knew in training knew where he was going or what his assignment would be in Vietnam. While I knew some other individuals from my home community were in Vietnam, I didn't know where they were, and I certainly wasn't in touch with them. We had been sent to Vietnam as individual replacements and each person individually assigned. I didn't know what I was getting into....but I was certainly concerned.

I almost missed hearing my name read since the orders were not issued in the standard Army alphabetical order that I was used to. Much to my shock, and initial disbelief, I was at the top of the order list. My assignment was to the 101st Airborne Division (Airmobile) in I Corps.

Orders - to the 101st Airborne Division in I Corps

Now I knew where I was going but I didn't know what awaited me! In late 1969, most Americans were quite aware of the

101st Airborne division's role in the retaking of Hue, and its more recent activities including Hamburger Hill, since both but particularly, Hamburger Hill, in all its bloody detail, had been prominently covered in the press about the time I was entering the Army. (The famous photographs of bloody, bandaged troopers, including medics, were recognized for what they were - classic photographs of the horror of war.) Once in the Army, we heard all about the 101st and its long tradition, from veterans of the division who had returned from a tour in Vietnam to serve as training officers or drill sergeants.

It was clear to me that I was being ordered up there because the division had a shortage of medics due to heavy casualties. On the order list going with me to the 101st were many other 91A10's - in fact, it seemed like almost everyone who was being assigned to the 101st Airborne was either a 91A10, or an 11B10 (the infantry MOS).

An Unexpected Epiphany

Following receipt of the orders sending me to the 101st, along with the other replacements who had been assigned to the division, I went through additional in-country processing in Long Binh. Then, after the inevitable period of waiting for hours during a very hot day, toward dusk we marched - carrying all our gear - into a waiting C-130 . Inside we sat in hammock style rope seats along the sides of the cargo bay with pallets of cargo strapped down in the middle. The plane took off heading north on a long uncomfortable (all night) flight. With the exception of those few soldiers who were back for a second tour with the division, most of us were uneasy about the unknown. We did not really know what we were flying

appreciated by others and that they would pay him for his skills. Writing in January 1862, in the letter from Fort Monroe quoted on the previous page:

...One night the captain wanted me to go up in his quarters and stop awhile. I went up and he got me to take a sketch of our pilot and I did. He was much pleased with it and he showed it all around to the offficrs, colonels, and lieutenant colonels and all and they said that it was first rate and they wanted me to stay all night and I did and got a first rate breakfast in the morning to pay. I am going to sketch the fort for him....

(Vintage, pgs 39 and 40.)
It would have life-long consquences.

Eugene had been shipped south as part of the large buildup of Union troops at the mouth of the Mississippi River after New Orleans had been taken by the Federal Navy under Admiral Farragut.

toward, but each of us was thinking about it. After some desultory conversation while we were taking off, everyone was silent for most of the night, dozing or thinking private thoughts as we flew through the night, landing shortly after dawn at the Phu Bai Airport, just south of Hue.

In my short first letter from Vietnam dated December 10, 1969 to my parents, my mood was guarded and I offered my parents a very brief and terse account of my journey so far:

Dec 10

> *Just a short note to let you know I arrived. Am way up north near Hue. With the 101st Airborne Division - don't use the address on the envelope as it will change shortly. I'm going thru more training. I'm not sure how this is going to work out. Needless to say I don't like it.*
> *I can't really say too much because I haven't been here long enough (Phu Bai is the specific place). I was near Saigon for two days as my plane from Oakland landed at Long Bien (Bien Hoa airport). The flight over took 16 hrs and I lost a day (left Oakland on the 6th and landed on the 8th!)*
> *A weird way to come to war - flying a commercial flight - being served meals, etc by pretty stewardesses - and sitting there in your jungle fatigues!*

As we deplaned at Phi Bai I had one of the most amazing experiences of my life - it involved an insight of such profundity that it was almost as if I had experienced an epiphany. When the cargo doors were lowered and we marched into bright sunlight, I marched out into a Chinese Landscape painting, and

I was overwhelmed by this sudden understanding of Chinese art. (Here I probably need to add a short explanation for most readers: When I had taken art history in college, among the subjects I studied in art history were the arts of Asia, particularly the painting of China. Because the Chinese have such a long history of landscape painting, a good deal of our time in that class was spent on this particular subject. Most traditional Chinese painting, I was told, is not naturalistic - as in the western sense. My art history teachers taught me that Chinese painting was a stylized way of rendering the landscape - not a

Insignia and namepatch

realistic way.)

When I walked out into that moist monsoon landscape in Phu Bai, under the diffuse sunlight that only the monsoon provides, I had never seen light and foliage like that in my life. Beyond the bunkers and barbed wire surrounding the airport, bamboo leaves flickered in the gentle breeze and the bright emerald green of the newly planted rice almost glowed with an unreal luminosity. In the distance, over the tops of the monsoon clouds, rose the mountains, and my thoughts moved away from the war I had come to participate in and back to long forgotten moments in darkened art history classrooms looking at dim slides of Chinese paintings. "My god, " I thought, "Those art history teachers didn't know what they were talking about - they really didn't know anything about Chinese landscape painting.... " I was looking at a Chinese landscape painting - the mountains did rise out of the monsoon clouds, and the bamboo leaves did rustle in the breeze just as the artists had rendered them, and there was even a brightly colored warbler (I believe it was a warbler) that looked like some of the birds that I remembered as having been so wonderfully depicted on silk with just a few skillful brush strokes by those masters. I understood: Chinese painters were truly naturalistic in their paintings - it was just that their landscape and their conventions of representations were so different from ours. My teachers hadn't ever understood that, but now I did.

After that insight, during which those brief moments provided me with a reverie, the thought was pushed out of my consciousness before it could be fully savored or appreciated. It was replaced by the immediacies of my situation. While the circumstances quickly pushed it out of my immediate consciousness (it was gone before I really had a chance to savor it), that instant remains in my memory as one of those rare moments in one's

Looking west from Pui Bai

life when one reaches an understanding with the instantaneousness of a blinding flash of light. It remains one of those rare moments in my life when I experienced such a powerful insight and a vision that gave me a complete understanding of a concept in a way not only notable for its clarity and power, but also for its profundity. (It is also one of my most incongruous memories of Vietnam.)

It didn't last long, but was replaced with the inevitable reality of standing in line, responding to a shouted request for name, rank, and serial number, (followed by "Sir" since I was being addressed by a lieutenant). I was back in the Army on my way to war instead of in my art history class.

Next, of course, it was time for filling out forms and talking to clerks and waiting to be processed one more time. But as I did

On the Perfume river.

The Cathedral of Hue.

those things, when I could look at the land that surrounded me, I was fascinated and possessed by its beauty. For a brief time my apprehensions about what lay ahead of me were banished. I just reveled in the beauty of the land. My introduction to the beauty of Vietnam was such a powerful experience that it gave me an insight not ever to be forgotten.

After that inevitable processing at the Phu Bai airport, we were loaded onto the back of "duce and a half" trucks for the ride north to Camp Evans, where we would receive another round of training and orientation specific to the 101st Airborne. The 90th Replacement Battalion in Long Bin/Bin Hoa had assigned me to the Division, and so there I was in Phu Bai, but I still didn't know specifically where I would go within it - the division would assign me where I was most needed. I wasn't feeling very good about my options. While there were a few options that I was aware of, I thought that the most likely one was assignment to an infantry company. The NVA had learned the value of undercutting the morale of US troops by deliberately taking out the medics whenever possible. Very early in our training we had been taught that we would be singled out as primary targets by the NVA right along with officers, NCO's and radio operators. Unlike WWII, where Army medical personnel wore red crosses prominently displayed on their sleeves, we wore nothing that would identify us as medical personnel.

Some background

Phu Bai was the American controlled airbase just south of Hue, the old Imperial Capital of Vietnam, a city second only to Saigon in size and importance. Hue had been a beautiful city, spread out along the Perfume River (which smelled like anything except perfume) but the battle for control of Hue had left it devastated. Taken by the VC and NVA during the Tet Offensive in 1968, it had been held for almost 60 days during which time a large number of local officials had been rounded up and executed. Vietnamese troops along with US Marines and Airborne units retook the city only after weeks of savage fighting, including bitter house to house combat. The 101st Airborne Division had initially been sent North to I Corps to provide reinforcement troops as the fighting for Hue seemed to be winding down. As it turned out, the 101st Airborne took almost as many casualties as the Marines had suffered during their time there. The final fighting for control was fierce as the NVA fought to the end.

When I arrived, Hue was still in a terrible state. Although the rebuilding of the city was slowly progressing, much of it was still in ruins even as life began to return to some semblance of normalcy. (The South Vietnamese government was very eager to restore the historic sections of the city as well as rebuild its economy since the city had such a prominent role in the history of the country of Vietnam.) The city had many historic

Ship Island

Eugene finally arrived at Ship Island off the coast of Missippi near the head of the Missippi River on February 13, 1862 , after turning back briefly, hence losing a few days. His total time in transit from Lowell was over a month - almost 5 weeks, in fact.

He, like I, also encountered a exotic landscape; the southern and brilliantly hot white sandy beaches and the gentle warm waters of the Gulf of Mexico were a far cry from the rocky cold and stormy coast of Maine. Until entering the Army, Eugene had never been out of Maine so the island must have been as awesome for him as Vietnam was for me. White beaches and warm ocean water in February - Eugene must have felt he had landed in a heavenly paradise in so far as the climate was concerned. Just as I still remember my vision at Phu Bai, it must have been something he remembered the rest of his life .

Eugene's letters home in these days convey no doubts about his decision to enlist and he finished his journey South in high spirits. In a letter to his mother he wrote (in part):

Ship island, February 13, 1862

Dear Mother,

We are here at last and I can ashure (sic) you that we are glad of it. We arrived and landed yesterday and have now got our tents pitched and ready to commence operations in the way of drilling. We had a splendid voyage of it and met with no mishaps on our way with one exception and that I will tell....

...There are several other islands in sight and we can see the shores of the main land of north about seven miles very distinctly. It is real warm here and we go around in our shirt sleeves some barefoot and with straw hats on. A lot of the boys went in bathing this morning and said the water was quite warm. I think I shall like here first rate after we get settled in our camp for the first impression is good...

(Vintage, pgs 49 and 50)

buildings, including the Old Citadel which had housed the government offices. The Government was eager to try to restore them as quickly as possible.

After the city of Hue was retaken, the Marines moved north to Quang Tri Province as the 101st Airborne took over the responsibilities for Thui Thien province which stretched West to the A Shau valley and the border with Laos little more than 20 miles away. South Vietnam was very narrow at this point and the coastal plain was even narrower. But it was there that most of the population was concentrated and since the war had now entered its Vietnamization stage in 1969, the division now had the task of pacification and civic action to go along with its more traditional combat role.

My Journey Continues

In the second half of my first letter, dated a day later, I described my first hours in I Corps and the beauty of the people and the landscape:

Dec 11

Went on a convoy thru Hue today then to another base camp for training. Which is where I am now. (Camp Evans) At first...Vietnam seems peaceful but war scars are everywhere-as are troops and military vehicles. Military dress is everywhere-on civilians as well as soldiers!

However it's wet - and cold! And I don't even have a field jacket! (I had to turn it in at processing in the South!) So - I may ask you to send something if I don't get issued something at my unit.

The landscape is fantastic at times - for instance now, during the monsoon, the mountains do rise up-

not from the ground but from the mist & the clouds. Just as the Chinese painters portrayed them.

The Vietnamese people are very handsome - very small but delicately handsome. Graves and ancestral altars/temples dot the landscape. Some are even inside these ugly base camps (forts) the army puts up - scared raw earth & tin roofed barracks with sand-bagged bunkers scattered around the ring of barbed wire that surrounds the forts.

Two days later I was still trying to find the time to finish the letter.

Dec 13

...Whenever you send anything that might be soiled or ruined by moisture put it inside a plastic bag and seal it. I could use some plastic bags anyway. Not much more to say at this point except that its going to be one damn long year.

Also that I'm running out of reading material.

Andy

I wanted reading material because, even though I was in Vietnam and there was a war going on, there were still long periods of that time-honored, Army practice known as " hurry up and wait". And, I wanted to read as I waited.

Ship Island, now a National Park had been first used as a military base by the British during the War of 1812. A Union fort had been partially constructed by 1861 but that was occupied by the Mississippi militia at the beginning of the Civil War. Retaken and used as a staging area while Farragut's fleet assaulted the cities defenses and captured New Orleans, the island served as a resupply base for General Butler's union troops who occupied New Orleans on May 1, 1862.

Writing his mother :

New Orleans, May 9, 1862

Dear Mother,

Would you think of it? We are right here in the heart of the Southern Confederacy and have not seen a brush yet. We started from Ship Island last Sunday, but I will go back a little I guess. A week ago our company and two others of our Regt. got orders to embark and go over to Fort Pike near Lake Ponshateram(I believe it is spelled so) [Ponchartrain] *and attack it. So we packed up our things and marched down to the warf about 9 o'clock at night and after waiting about an hour we got orders to march back and go with the Regt. which was to leave for Orleans . New Orleans had been taken about two weeks before by our fleet and we were to go there for guards and to keep the city down. So last Sunday we started on board the rebel prize Tennessee a large steamship. We sailed about 9 o'clock at night and anchored for we had some freight aboard for the Mass. Regt. which was there. We did not get off until the next day about noon so we had some time to look around from the ship and see the forts all battered down by our shot and shell. We could see the fire rafts and sunken gunboats of the enemy all around and some of their contrivances looked kind of ugly I can tell you. The afternoon we sailed up the Mississippi was a splendid one. It was cool and balmy as you could wish and I never enjoyed myself more in my life it seems to me. The first night on shore our company was detailed to guard the upper part of the city about three miles from our Regt. and here we now are. This part of the city is called Jefferson City. We were detailed because we was the best company on the ground and we have got the best chance there is. We are in rooms over a billiard hall and drinking saloon and we have first rate*

A Historical Digression on the 101st Airborne Division and Vietnam

I later learned that, when I arrived in December 1969, the 101st, famed for its exploits in Europe during World War II, had been in Vietnam as a full division for just two years although the 1st Brigade of the Division had been in Vietnam since 1965. The division had just completed its conversion from a paratroop division to one of the two, newly created, innovative and elite Army Airmobile divisions. The Airmobile concept, built on the then recently recognized capabilities of the helicopter, was truly innovative at that time. The other air mobile US Army division was the 1st Cavalry Division (Airmobile), and both divisions needed a huge allocation of expensive helicopters to fulfill their role. The 1st Air Cavalry was the first to receive the helicopters and was fully constituted as an airmobile division in 1965. By the time I arrived the official conversion of the 101st Airborne Division to Airmobile was complete, and the Division was now organized around the helicopter. So instead of deploying and delivering troops and supplies via parachute, they were now delivered and supported by helicopter. While that tactical innovation, revolutionary as it was, didn't change the nature of the war, nor the balance of power, it made it possible for the US to hold its own (for a time) against a determined enemy with far more numerous (although less well equipped) troops.

Writing in the introduction to *After Tet*, Ronald Spector notes that:

> *...the most appropriate analogy to Vietnam is World*

War I. As in World War I on the Western Front, the war in Vietnam was a stalemate and had been a stalemate since the early months of the conflict. As in World War I, neither side was prepared to admit this fact, and each side grossly underestimated the determination and staying power of the other....
(Spector pg. XVI)

And while the analogy to WWI may initially seem incongruous, it is probably quite appropriate. At the time, the introduction of new technology in the form of the helicopter made new tactics possible and appeared to many American military strategists to solve one of the vexing problems of the Vietnamese war for the United States. This was: How to win a war against an enemy who did not marshal his resources to stand and fight in a fixed battle, but rather yielded ground, dispersing troops when appropriate, only to mass them when the opportunity to attack presented itself? And, then repeated the process again and again.

In Vietnam, the US chose to try and solve this problem with the use of both the airmobile divisions, the 1st Air Cavalry and the 101st Airborne Division, in areas that could not otherwise be controlled without a massive infusion of additional American troops. By 1969, with Richard Nixon's election and promise to end the war, a massive infusion of troops was politically impossible since this would have required calling up the reserves to provide the numbers required which were far beyond the approximately 550,000 already deployed in Vietnam at the time of my arrival along with many thousands more supporting the effort from bases in Thailand, the Philippines or on ships at sea. The airmobile divisions could control vast areas by constantly inserting troops and artillery support at the crudely constructed firebases which were constantly

times. We have the liberty to go all over the city and see the sights and we improve the opportunity you may guess. The poorest classes are all starving and there is no business scarcely. We find a good many union people here and also a good many secessionists and negros in plenty. One will find two drinking houses here where you find one store of any other kind and gambling is all the go but our captain does not allow his boys to drink and if he catches them at it he punishes them by giving them extra drill. there are thousands of things I would like to tell you about but I must wait until i get home I suppose. I am well and so are all the rest of the boys and we have very few sick in the Regt. I cannot stop to write more now for I am in a great hurry. I will write again soon.

Eugene Kingman
P.S. I hope to see home soon.

In a letter to his father a month later:

Dear Father,
I do not know but what you have been worried about me because I have not written oftener but for the last three weeks to day I have been sick in the hospital down to New Orleans

with an attack of Pleursy Fever but I am better now and returned to duty up here to our quarters at Jefferson City. I came up yesterday. The first week I was down there I was pretty sick but for the last two weeks I have only stayed down there because I was too weak to do duty. .....We do not suffer a great deal from the heat here not so much as I have at home in June but the mosquitos are awful thick and large and bloodthirsty and in the hospital the beds were furnished with mosquito nets...
(Vintage pg. 76)

This was an omen of things to come. As we know, disease took a huge toll of soldiers on both sides of the Civil War. I believe it claimed more lives than combat.

being built and were designed to be occupied only briefly, then abandoned at very short notice - perhaps to be reoccupied in the indefinite future as needed. These bases, located within supporting distance of each other formed a constantly shifting grid that provided interlocking and mutually reinforcing artillery fire support over a wide area - and, because of the mobility that the helicopter provided, occupancy and support could be shifted according to need. This theoretically allowed the 101st to effective counter the force of the NVA, estimated at two or three times our numbers in the province of Thua Tien. It was a strategy that worked extremely well when the use of the technology was applied flawlessly - but if it wasn't used with skill and understanding the cost could be heavy .

It now seems clear to me that since the US never adequately prepared the South Vietnamese government and its armed forces to take over this strategy as our commitment was phased out - or to develop an appropriate alternative - their attempts to follow our methods failed. In hindsight, it seems that those critics of the war were right when they said that following the initial US involvement in Vietnam, successive US governments had all failed to plan for the time when the US military would leave and the war would be returned to the Vietnamese people.

However that might play out in the future, the helicopter in all its various permutations, was central to the US war strategy and almost ubiquitous in my existence there. In the 101st, helicopters came in many varieties: the large, twin engined, dual rotored, troop carrying CH-47 Chinooks; the smaller, single engined, all-purpose Hueys which transported troops, cargo and carried us around much of the time; the tiny two-person OH-6 LOH's (or Loachs as they were referred to); light observation helicopters and the newly introduced AH-6 Cobras, sleek, heavily armed modifications of the Huey that carried an impressive array of guns, grenade launchers and rockets in any variety of proportions. Additionally, on occasion, we would see special purpose helicopters such as the CH-63 Sky Cranes which were designed for lifting heavy objects and which looked like giant insects with their long legs extended, legs that were proportioned to fit around steel containers. The Marines and Air Force used other varieties of helicopters for their specialized missions as well.

I Corps was the northern most military region in the Republic of South Vietnam and stretched from the Demilitarized Zone southward to and including the province of Quang Ngai where the Central Highlands of Vietnam began. The 101st Airborne was then deployed in several large bases, and many smaller fire bases spread out in an arc north and west of the city of Hue.

The 101st Airborne, with its headquarters at Camp Eagle where I was soon to be assigned, also had a very large number of troops at Camp Evans, north of Hue, where I was now to undergo my intense and very real "in-country" training . The division provided the security for Thua Thien Province including

The remains of houses along the Pertume River

An OH-6 LOH(Loach)

the "blocking" of access from the NVA strongholds in the A Shau Valley to Hue . The division provided this security by supporting the ARVN troops in the province and operating a fluid number of small fire support bases (firebases) west of Hue. Both efforts were aimed at blocking the access routes east from the A Shau, and both were supported by the larger bases of Eagle and Evans.

North of Thua Thien, the Marines had the same blocking assignment in Quang Tri Province, the northernmost province of South Vietnam where they were spread as a defensive force running roughly along an arc from the sea inland along the DMZ to the northern hills, reaches and valleys running into the A Shau where the borders of North Vietnam, South Vietnam and Laos converged in very rugged country. The Marines lacked the level of helicopter support that the fully airmobile 101st had, and so they practiced a slightly different strategy that depended more on fixed firebases such as Khe Sanh and on aggressive patrols, supported by massive air power from Navy ships based offshore in the South China Sea and by B-52's in Thailand as well as by heavy artillery.

I didn't know much about the area around Hue, except that it was in a region referred to by the US military as I Corps, and I knew it included the Au Shau Valley. In those days the name Au Shau Valley invoked a vision of a place of unspeakable terrors. It was described by the press as consisting of almost mythical triple canopy jungle that produced a forbidding darkness inhabited by a dauntingly deadly enemy and filled with the prospect of almost certain doom. The Au Shau Valley ran north and south behind a string of forbidding mountains between Laos and South Vietnam. For years, reports had been regularly coming out of Vietnam about the significance to the North Vietnamese war effort of the Ho Chi Minh Trail, a road

The military designations for South Vietnam

(actually multiple roads and paths) that wound down under the cover of triple canopy jungle, from the valleys of southwestern North Vietnam through Laos and into South Vietnam. Its many branches were built, rebuilt, defended and maintained during the war. Since this route was so important to the resupply efforts by the North, not only was it regularly bombed by the US with B-52's, but the floor of the valley had been (and continued to be) hotly contested, with regularity. I knew a number of bloody, and newsworthy, battles had been fought in and around the valley between the NVA and US /ARVN forces - initially by US Special Forces and Montagnard troops but more recently by regular US Marines and Army Airborne troops.

These included the siege of Khe Sanh in early 1968 and the bloody seizure of Hue; both had already become part of the mythology of the war in Vietnam. The recently concluded battle of Hamburger Hill (Ap Bia Mountain) was yet another event in the bloody crescendo of actions that I knew took place in the northern part of South Vietnam during the years of 1968-69. (Of course, there were many, many bloody encounters that never made the news.)

Along with the interdiction efforts in the Au Shau and surrounding area, the 101st had been given the assignment of providing protection for the city of Hue and pacifying Thua Thien province. The interdiction effort (which ultimately proved to be futile) aimed at preventing the NVA from using the Au Shau valley as an infiltration, support and resupply route from the North to the South was a major focus of the Division during the 1st half of 1969. We now know, that for much of 1969, while the 101st had devoted a great deal of its effort to the interdiction effort, mounting several incursions into the Au Shau as well as building fire support bases, LZ's (landing zones) and extending highway 547 west from Phu Bai and Hue, the effort failed. In

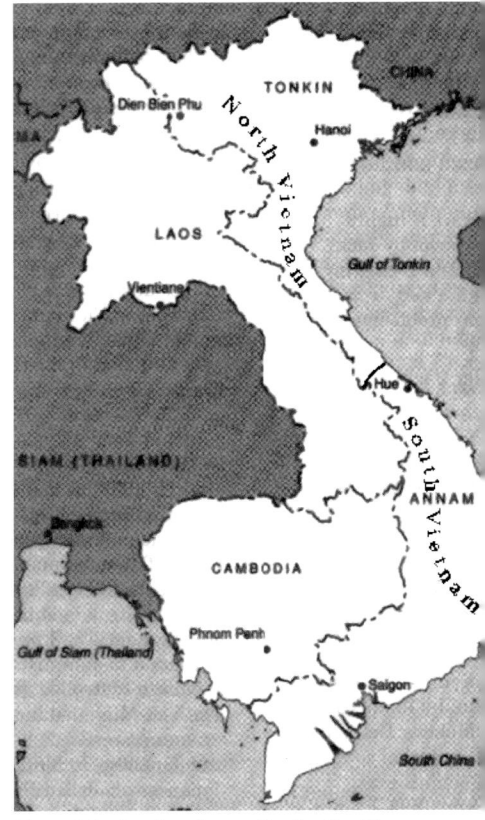

Map of the Region: Laos, Cambodia, Vietnam (North & South)

retrospect, it now seems clear that the effort had proved largely futile since the North Vietnamese had simply shifted many of their supply lines west into Laos. Mounting American casualties (at places like Hamburger Hill) had generated bad publicity at home to an American public weary and disgusted at the seemingly endless war, and the Division was ordered to avoid picking bloody battles unless it became absolutely necessary. Richard Nixon had been elected President by promising to end the war in Vietnam and bring home the troops, and so, in early June of 1969, in an effort to keep his campaign promise, he announced the policy known as the "Vietnamization" of the war.

By late in 1969, this phase of the war - during which the ARVN forces would now be asked to carry the heaviest burden of the fighting with US troops playing a supporting role, was beginning to have its effects felt in the day-to-day operations. The effects of this changed strategy had become clearly evident by the late summer of 1969. Thus, by the time I got to Camp Eagle in December that year, the strategy and the method of operations not only for the 101st Airborne Division, but also for the whole US Army in Vietnam were significantly changed from the spring of that same year. According to this new policy, the US Army would focus on pacification in addition to providing support and training of the armed forces of South Vietnam.

Orientation to the 101st and in-country training

Camp Evans was located some miles northeast of Hue, not far from the Gulf of Tonkin of the South China Sea. The camp was just off of the old Route One - the historic highway running North and South all along the coast of Vietnam. Old Route One connected the major cities of the South to the northern cities of Da Nang and Hue. Then it headed north to Quang Tri City and beyond the DMZ into North Vietnam. Before the war, it had run all the way from Saigon to Hanoi. A narrow gauge railroad ran alongside the highway between Hue and Da Nang. Route One north of Hue ran parallel to another old French highway in Quang Tri province (closer to the sea) which was the highway referred to as the "Street Without Joy" that Bernard Fall was writing about on his last trip to Viet Nam when he lost his life.

Evans was a bleak and forbidding place of worn bunkers and weathered seahuts set in the middle of a great plain. We were arriving at the height of the monsoon season which made it even bleaker and more forbidding. Surrounded only by rice paddies and fields stripped of most of their vegetation, it seemed like I had been put into a kind of unimaginable nightmare, for in one critical way it was not like anything I had been trained to expect. I was expecting heat and a jungle. But I was cold - in fact I was shivering. This northern part of South Vietnam was a cold, wet, foggy, dreary and desolate place with temperatures in the 50's and 60's when I arrived.

During the peak of the monsoon the rains were almost constant and unbelievably heavy for long periods of time. For example, in one 36-hour period we had more rain than New York City got in an average year! (And I was told that wasn't bad: during one stretch before I got there they had gotten even heavier rain!) Without my field jacket (I cursed myself for giving it up) I was always cold those first days. The poncho and poncho liner combination I had been issued did little to keep me warm when I tried to sleep at night even though we did have a seahut to sleep in and were not sleeping on the ground. I slept in two uniforms and wrapped myself in the poncho and poncho

A Train on the way to Danang

liner but still had chattering teeth through the nights. It wasn't until I got to Camp Eagle that I was able to scrounge a field jacket and an extra poncho liner that made my life more comfortable. A month or so later, when someone in our company rotated out, I was finally able to secure a down sleeping bag. This was a prized possession.

All newcomers assigned to the 101st Airborne were given RVN refresher training at Camp Evans which was intense, realistic and specific to the Division. Along with the small unit tactics training complete with a patrol, the course included refresher weapons training. Of course, it was not a refresher course to me: as a conscientious objector I had never received weapons instruction in my basic training. Not knowing where I would be sent I thought it wouldn't hurt to complete the course. There was a good chance I might be assigned to an infantry company.

Growing up in rural Western New York State, an area with lots of hunting, I had plenty of familiarity with weapons. My

A view of Camp Evans

common sense and commitment to self preservation convinced me that I should take the weapons course just in case! While I didn't plan on carrying a weapon since my job as a medic would have me focused on other things, I felt that I didn't have anything to lose by undergoing an introduction to the weapons that would be used by those around me. I had made the decision to become a conscientious objector based on my strong personal beliefs that I could not accept an order that forced me to take the life of another person in a cause that I did not believe in. However, I was not so pacifistic that I would not defend myself if I were put in a dire situation. If circumstances made it necessary, I would be able to pick up a weapon and use it in self defense.

From that perspective, it was easy to decide that I should take the weapons refresher course. For someone who had hunted extensively and had handled many different kinds of firearms for years from the time I was in my early teens, the weapons proved relatively simple to use. I fired the M16 rifle, the M60 machine gun and the M79 grenade launcher and threw hand grenades. After that I felt that if, in an emergency I needed to pick up a weapon, I could be reasonably proficient in the use of it. To my way of thinking, it was like taking out a life insurance policy.

The training did not, however, change my mind about my role or my beliefs.

In a letter to my sister Betsy and her husband Steve, I wrote:

Dec 15

Betsy & Steve

Somewhere I have the beginnings of a letter to you when I was in a slightly better humor about being in the 101st Airborne-that's right paratroopers! But after three days of hearing about how to kill "umpteen" ways I'm a bit fed up with them -(only 355 days to go!) Maybe when I get to my unit it will be better....
About half of the men here are real killers-they really want to shoot a "gook" as they call the Vietnamese. (I'm sure these guys will be damned good soldiers!).... Wrote this while I was in training & surrounded by trigger happy troopers.

On a patrol that was part of the training, it became crystal clear that many of the soldiers were filled with bravado and enthusiasm for the task - whether that was innocent or not wasn't apparent in those days. But as the letter indicated, I wasn't happy about the eagerness of many of the soldiers to enter into the business of killing so willingly and eagerly. I accepted the fact that the Army was there to fight a war, and the division's business was about killing. However, because of the enthusiasm of those "trigger happy troopers" the 101st Airborne Division had earned a well deserved, and proudly borne, reputation for its willingness to do battle with the enemy. The division 's troopers were very aggressive in carrying out or initiating actions and because the Viet Cong and the NVA were formidable opponents - equally tough, committed and willing to stand and do battle - the division took heavy casualties . In this war the medics were priority targets and in the months preceding my arrival had suffered high casualty rates. As replacements, we may not have been eager to enter the killing fields, but most, including me, were ready to do our duty, whatever our reservations.

After the few days of "In Country" training at Evans (combined with many hours of guard duty, both day and night), I learned where my permanent assignment would be: the HHC of the 101st Aviation Group at Camp Eagle. (Not that I knew then what that assignment meant.) After getting my orders, on a day when the monsoon rains were pouring down so hard that all helicopters were grounded, we were loaded on the backs of "duce and a half" trucks, where we sat under a leaking canvas covers and headed back down Rt. 1 past Hue, where we turned off near the village of My Thu Phuong and headed toward Camp Eagle.

While doing some research in preparation for the writing of this account, I discovered that the village of My Thu Phuong had previously been home to a sizable number of National Liberation Front cadres who had been repatriated from the north years earlier and who became active in the Tet Offensive of 1968. It must have seemed the height of irony that the 101st established a sizable base camp just down the road, and, since many people from the village were employed on Camp Eagle, it must have offered a wonderful opportunity for them to get intelligence on our operations and capabilities.

But of course I knew nothing about this as I disembarked from a "duce and a half" at the sea hut that served as the clerical headquarters for the 101st Aviation Group. At the time I arrived, I had no idea of what the Aviation Group consisted of or how it operated within the Division.

Chapter 3 Camp Eagle

HHC Dispensary/HHC 101st Avn Group

Once I was settled in at the dispensary my existence became more clearly outlined. There were several aspects to my assignment. The main one was working in the dispensary, where I subsequently acquired several responsibilities. One part of my job included going on medcaps, those combined US/ARVN medical team visits to villages as part of the civic action program. I also went on patrols as the medic about once a week, and we all coped with unanticipated emergencies that frequently came up.

A Chinook over Eagle - from my sketchbook

By the end of my first month with the 101st, things had begun to settle into a pattern. I wrote to my sister and Steve:

Jan 26

Betsy & Steve,
Glad to hear from you - from Greene St. no less! [Note, B & S had just moved into, and were renovating a wonderful loft on Greene Street in the Soho section of NYC.]
Not much to report from here! The sun is out for the first time in a month and it's now red dust instead of red mud.
The work is now routine, most of the time dull. Although every now and then something of interest

Camp Eagle

happens. Like the other evening when I did my first suturing. Or when we drew automatic weapons fire - briefly! Nothing serious. Have gone on another Medcap - which was enjoyable except that I gave all the shots & that included some young infants! Needless to say I don't like poking a needle in a kid's ass when he's (or she's) kicking and screaming! Adults don't bother me - they just wince! Seriously, I really am scared when I give shots to kids.

 Have started taking some pictures with a half frame camera I got (Olympus Pen FT) but plan to buy a Canon FT QL with this paycheck & then do more. The Pen is good to carry on a Medcap or a Patrol but the negatives are too small for a lot of work. Am only allowed to buy two (still) cameras here (we have ration cards) so I'm sort of sorry I bought the Pen! However back in the world I can always sell it for what I paid here!

 Would you send me Donnie Jo's [Steve's sister's] address, I have a card & note from her but no return address! (Also perhaps the correct spelling of her married name!) She sent it to my Texas address and believe it or not, it got to me almost two weeks before one from Almond mailed to the 101 Replacement Det! (It arrived yesterday!)

 A noisy night tonight, the Cobras (helicopter gunships) are all over the place. By the way I do enjoy flying in helicopters - every time I've been up (in a Huey) they've flown with the doors open (& once I rode where one of the side gunners sits), when they bank sharply the only thing holding you in is the safety belt! One enjoys what one can over here!....

 For instance: Budweiser Beer is highly prized over here - not so much for its taste (although I prefer it) but because it comes in all aluminum cans! Most other

Repair facilities with Cobras

Inside a Huey

beers have steel cans - which rust! Little things like that become important.

And I'm going to call it quits before I get too mad! Hope the loft is shaping up.

Andy

The HHC Company dispensary where I worked served the various units of the 101st Aviation Group. This included headquarters staff, and the staff of the Tactical Operations Center that contained the equipment manned by the communications and intelligence group coordinating the air operations of the Division. HHC had its own squadron of light observation helicopters (Loach's), so the pilots and mechanics as well as the Pathfinders who were part of the HHC of the 101st Aviation Group for those were also served. In addition to the above, since the 101st Avn. Group coordinated the operations of its subordinate units, the 101st Avn. Bn (AH), the 158th Avn. Bn., the 159 Avn. Bn., and the 163rd Avn. Co.(which constituted about half of the Division's helicopter operations), the dispensary served most of those units as well. HHC also had a motor pool for our trucks and jeeps as well as a mess hall in addition to the Group Headquarters buildings, dispensary and the various sleeping quarters. This organizational grouping was an indication of how technologically sophisticated the Army had become in its Airmobile Divisions. Most of the buildings were sandbagged Seahuts, except for the TOC (which was an underground bunker) or the mess hall and the shop maintenance buildings for helicopters. There were bunkers next to or nearby most buildings. All the helicopters were parked in revetments that partially protected them from incoming rockets or mortar fire.

The medical team for the HHC 101st Avn. Group had new medical responsibilities for the Division growing out of the evolution into an airmobile division. With the role and organization of the Group dispensary still evolving, the dispensary was staffed in a manner reflecting these new responsibilities and was not typical of a dispensary for other companies in the Division. It consisted of the medics assigned to the HHC company, (including the Pathfinder medics) as well as some medics assigned to the subordinate units and then forwarded from them and attached to the HHC dispensary. Also, some of us were there initially in unauthorized lines. I was initially assigned to the 101st Avn Group HHC, the headquarters company in an unauthorized slot, and then, halfway through my stay I was put in an authorized medics slot with the 163rd Aviation Company and then attached back to the HHC dispensary. The doctor in charge of the dispensary was not an ordinary M.D. He was a flight surgeon - a specialist in flight medicine. The flight surgeon oversaw the Aviation Group medical needs and in particular maintained the health of the pilots and other flight personnel. Because of the special medical needs of flight this was a medical specialty requiring, in particular, an understanding of the way medical treatments (including drugs) interacted with flying capabilities. But specialists like these were hard to find. (Capt. M. the initial flight surgeon, was there when I arrived and left in April while Capt. B. arrived later in early June. In between, and then after Capt. B. left in August, there were some long months when we didn't have a doctor in residence.) Our other professionally trained medical Specialist was Spec 5 (later Spec 6) Dave J., who was attached to the HHC Avn Group Dispensary from the 326th Medical Battalion (the 101st Airborne Division's medical battalion) as the senior NCO. Then there were about (it varied according to date) six 91B20's, the garden variety army medic, of which I was one.

Eugene's Early Days in Louisiana

Eugene's war was very different in many respects from mine. While he went to war in an exotic southern culture, he still remained among in his own country where the language and the culture had commonalities. By and large he fought in a war where there were battle fronts and secured territory, although there were guerrillas operating at all times during the Civil War. He lived in various places, in commandeered quarters some of the time, other times pitching camp while the Army was on the march. Still other times he was billeted in towns or cities, including some months in New Orleans where he mingled freely among the population.

Writing to his mother from New Orleans in a letter dated May 9:

...The first night on shore our Regt. passed in a cotton press, a large building where they press it for exporting. The next morning our company detailed to guard the upper part of the city about three miles from the Regt. and here we now are....We are in rooms over a billiard hall and drinking saloon and we have first rate

times. We have the liberty to go all over the city and see the sights and we improve the oportunity you may guess. The poorest classes here are all starving and there is no business doing scarcely...(Vintage, pg. 75)

Whenever they occupied new quarters they attempted to make themselves comfortable, and he often wrote home about how successful they had been and how comfortable were their quarters.

Writing his brother from New Orleans on August 3, 1862, he writes:

...We have moved from our old quarters in the mint and now our company is quartered in Louisiana Hall, a splendid place painted up and lit with gas throughout. It is in the 2nd story and has 13 large windows in it which run down to the floor and may be shoved up and used for doors to go out onto the balcony which runs around the building. In short it is a very nice place and I like it better than the Mint for it is more open and cool...
(Vintage, pg. 100)

Listed below are some of my fellow soldiers mentioned later in the text. Roger and Bruce were in the same group of replacements as I was and we arrived at the dispensary in the back of the same truck and worked together until I left.

Randy - the farmboy from South Dakota, very nice, good natured, worked hard and couldn't wait to get home to his small town.

Dave - the ranking Spec 5 (later Spec 6) NCO in charge of the Dispensary; a former emergency medical technician and the only medical pro (besides the doctors) among us, and very, very competent.

Royce - the resident Med Cap Specialist when I arrived in Group - very religious and a dedicated pacifist - but he bequeathed me a very large and exceedingly sharp knife on his DEROS (Date of Expected Return from Overseas Service).

Charlie - the pathfinder medic and a baby faced Rambo; his angelic looks belied his toughness

Roger - a Colorado farm boy who couldn't wait to return to the farm, he kept a sense of humor, did his job without complaining and would always lend a helping hand.

Jaster - a lanky, big boned high energy guy who couldn't stay still. He preferred patrols to working in the dispensary; upon his DEROS left me his pistol.

Bruce - a normally quiet almost taciturn, religious person who entered the Army a CO. Somewhere in training he was converted into a rather bellicose war enthusiast who, after Royce's DEROS, took over the Medcap's whenever he could.

Jim - from North Carolina, nervous and wiry, a chain smoker and worrier who worked the system bureaucratically and got us all in authorized slots so we wouldn't be snatched by an infantry company.

Dr. M. (Captain)- a fine doctor who taught us lots about medicine and was easy to work under. He went home early (in April 1970) after his wife suffered a medical emergency.

Dr. R (Captain) - our second flight surgeon arrived in mid-June and only stayed for a couple of months

Capt. G (later Major) - Helicopter pilot (OH-6 loach) for the HHC Avn Group -also served as a boy scout volunteer/sponsor while in Vietnam.

While the special medical focus of the dispensary was on the flight personnel, the broader medical responsibilities of the dispensary included the care of all the personnel of the entire 101st Avn Group, including its subordinate units. Pilots and crew members of helicopters regularly required flight physicals every three months. These were specialized physicals, tailored to the demands of flying, and, after some specialized training we all assisted in the administering of these activities. Of course, we also had the responsibilities of caring for the ongoing daily medical needs which included soldiers getting sick, hurt or wounded. Additionally, we administered the required shots and vaccinations to the units since soldiers in Vietnam required a huge number of vaccinations against the diseases prevalent there. We also took care of most of the medical emergencies in the Group dispensary. These included all kinds of problems from minor bullet wounds (seldom) to shrapnel wounds (frequently), to accidents, diseases, infections, and burns. We saw some of those every day. Soldiers, who were in need of more intense medical care were evacuated on an emergency basis to the 326th Medical Field Hospital.

Living Conditions on Eagle

The working and living conditions on Eagle were generally what "people back in the world" (our term for America) would have considered quite primitive. None-the-less, compared to troops assigned to the small fire bases, many of us felt lucky and considered our circumstances very comfortable - even palatial! Having said that, I need to make it clear that we had no running water, no indoor plumbing - no heat or, equally as important, no air conditioning. Everyone was billeted in a plywood seahut (a hootch) with a tin roof. Those kept us dry but the breeze blew in through the screen making it cold in the damp winter monsoon season and sweltering in the summer. We closed off the screen with canvas during the monsoon to keep the worst of the cold damp air from blowing in. We had cots to sleep on and nets to keep the mosquitos away. We had limited amounts of electricity most of the time, although it was not very powerful or dependable since it came from a small diesel generator the HHC Company maintained. This meant that in the hootches we were lucky to each have a single twin outlet in our assigned area which limited the things we could

Two views of Eagle, The photo on the left rhows the "Berm" line.

connect ; for example, I could plug in my fan and a desk light at the same time - but not my radio! Because of the communications and intelligence needs of the HHC, we had more dependable electricity than did many of the other units on Eagle all of whom operated their own generators.

Seahuts were the standard temporary buildings for American servicemen in Viet Nam and probably got their name from the fact that they were build by the Navy Seabees. They were constructed of unpainted plywood, with open studs built up off the ground about a foot, with a single sheet of plywood around the sides and were then screened the remaining two feet up to the eves that were about 6 feet high. The roof was a pitched to a central peak about 8 feet high but the trusses were little more than 6 1/2 feet high. During the winter monsoon season, when the screen was covered with a canvas tarp, it helped cut the cold wet wind and blown rain, but also kept the hootches dark. By the time I arrived at Eagle, the hootches all had metal roofs. Prior to that the roofs were all canvas.

The hootch where I slept was at the far end of the 101st Avn Group area, away from the dispensary but near the shower. Eight GI's were assigned to the hootch and all had personal living areas of about 6 x 8 feet which we each organized according to our individual needs although everyone tended to follow a similar pattern. Our hootch was largely, but not exclusively occupied by enlisted medics who were E-3's and E-4's. (Generally hootches were assigned according to job and rank.) Dave, our senior NCO, bunked in a different hootch with Sergeants, E-5's and E-6's. While they were the more senior enlisted personnel, they still had living conditions similar to ours. Each space in the seahuts had room for a cot and under the cot, under which we stored some of our personal belongings in a standard GI footlocker. Most of us also stored cases of soft drinks or beer under there as well. There was also a small refrigerator that we all shared and which kept sodas or beer cold - some of the time.

Getting comfortably settled in took a little time. As soldiers have done for centuries, I scavenged or had sent to me items that were needed to make my meager area more habitable. (Later, I read Eugene's letter home with considerable interest and discovered he did similar things.) The following note to my parents outlines my needs.

> *Jan 5*
>
> *Hi,*
> *This is just a note, an "I need" note.*
> *I need an extension cord with a socket for a bulb.*
> *Also a screw-in adaptor to make a receptacle from a*

The 101st Avn Group dispensary

light bulb socket.

Have asked Sean to send me a 1.3v mercury battery for a camera. Out in my studio, up in the painting racks there is a package of drawing paper (about 70 lb weight), I think its about 12" by 18' now - it probably could be rolled up (in a tube) and sent. My schedule is such that I'll get a chance to do some drawing (and have done some already) but my sketch books are too small for some things!

The weather is still terrible - rain, rain, and more rain..

Got a chance to go into Hue yesterday - not that I got out of the jeep - but I did see much from the jeep. All the cities & villages are "off limit" to the 101st! Why I don't know.

I'll be interested to hear from you - I understand there was quite a snow storm over the holidays!

Andy

I used the cord with a socket to build a clothes drying cabinet (a crude amoire) made from wooden rocket boxes that I scrounged nearby. Almost everyone built, bought or was given one of these "rocket box amoires". Outfitted with a bare light bulb at the bottom that was kept lighted most of the time - i.e., whenever the electricity was working - this created a warm dry space in which the heated air rose up by convection drying your clothing. This was the only way that clothes would dry after washing. The humidity during the monsoon season was so high that clothing would stay perpetually damp and gather mildew or would simply rot if left hanging in the dark, humid atmosphere of the hootch during those months when the canvas flaps were kept down and closed. It was also essential for drying your boots and socks which were perpetually soaked during the monsoon and frequently soggy during the "dryer" seasons. Since you were issued two pair of boots, you wore one pair while allowing the other pair to dry whenever possible. Socks were rotated very often - hopefully daily - and even twice a day if you got soaked on a patrol or Medcap. Socks were a prized item and most soldiers (all the medics) hoarded extra socks. We always kept at least one dry pair handy. (One of the things medics spent a lot of time treating the troops for was trenchfoot, a condition where the skin of the foot turned soft and white from constant exposure to water and then it began to peel off exposing the foot to fungal or bacterial infections. This was a condition which could - and frequently did - become very serious extremely quickly! A systemic infection could develop in a few hours - or the foot could even become gangrenous!)

Like most, I also built a crude desk using scavenged lumber from those same rocket boxes to write on as the writing of letters was a welcome escape from my reality and it frequently became an obsession. Reading was also a welcome exercise. Hence, the skillful use of a single outlet became an art form as we plugged and unplugged our light, fan and radio according to our activities or needs.

A metal folding chair was another prized item to be scrounged and, after it was acquired, was used on those times when I was off duty to read or write letters. My prized short wave radio ordered from the PX, allowed me to receive classical concerts from the BBC - and from Radio Moscow! The US Army radio stations played a very loud and raucous brand of rock and roll mixed with country music - sometimes more of the latter than the former. The radio was also the source of news from the Voice of America, the BBC, Australian stations, Radio Hanoi and Radio Moscow.

Acclimating (and not just to the weather)

We did not have running water, so water for drinking, washing and bathing was brought around by tanker truck every day to storage tanks set up in various places in the area. We filled our canteens, coolers and containers from those tanks as needed. Because the water was so bad - in its raw form it was very unsafe and dirty - it was heavily chlorinated to purify it. The result was water so laced with chlorine that the smell of chlorine overwhelmed you even before you drank. Thus, drinking water was usually mixed with a strong dose of Cool-Aid before you drank it or before filling canteens. Needless to say, I preferred to drink a lot of beer (warm) and/or soft drinks (warm). When we made coffee, we made very strong coffee, but even strong coffee could not disguise the chlorine. I never did get used to the water - but I did get quite used to drinking warm beer.

Lacking plumbing we used outhouses that we referred to as "shit houses". While I was previously familiar with outhouses since they were still found on a number of farms where I grew up, these had a somewhat unique and very unpleasant feature. Because the water table was so high, the outhouses were elevated. Instead of depositing the human waste in holes in the ground to be covered over, the human excrement was collected in barrels, removed daily, mixed with diesel fuel and burned. This resulted in a distinctive sickly sweet odor of burning feces and diesel fuel. If there were no breezes to blow it away, this unforgettable stench hung over the whole camp. (If you were downwind of an American base, you had no trouble locating it.)

Burning feces

During those first months in Louisiana life was still an adventure, so writing home on October 9, 1862 from Lake Port, Louisiana (a village on Lake Pontchartrain), Eugene boasts a little:

"...The railroad runs out to the end of the wharf and there are a number of baggage cars at the end of the route which they do not use and they make capital houses for 2, and Mell Gould and myself are together in one. I am commander of the post and it is our duty to overhaul all the boats that come in and all the boats that go out and see that they have got the proper passes and carry nothing that is contraband. We have to hail a good many oyster boats and other fishing craft and of course we make them fork over some of their cargo so we have any quantity of fish and oysters. The other day we found a man who had a revolver and powder with him so we confiscated his whole rig and we have flapjacks and sugar in quantit...."
(Vintage pg.119)

In January of 1863, he writes:

"Dear Father,

About two weeks ago we got orders to leave Lake Port and the day before

There was a shower house - sheets of plywood around an open area under a framework holding up a large elevated water tank which fed by gravity the shower heads installed beneath it. When I first got there, we showered under cold water, which - since it was the monsoon season and temperatures were in the 50's - was very cold water indeed! But a month or so after I arrived, the seabees rigged up a very clever gravity-fed heating unit that used dripping diesel fuel to heat the water for the shower during the rest of the monsoon season. After that heating unit was constructed the potential for a hot shower existed - although you had to time your shower just right because if you showered too soon after the fire was lit the water was still very cold, and if you waited too long the water became scalding. Unfortunately, and all too often, your duty assignment hours didn't allow for the luxury of timing your shower just perfectly, so usually it was cold - or scalding. Those few occasions when you timed it just right and the water was perfect, were memorable. You stayed in the warm shower as long as possible. In the summer, of course, we didn't have to heat the water as the tank would be heated almost to the boiling point by the sun. So, timing was still important, but you reversed the cycle and tried to shower shortly after it was

The shower house with hootchs

filled or it would quickly heat up. Unfortunately on many days it was still very hot at midnight. On other occasions during the summer, cooling off was so glorious after 110 degree days, that there were many nights when the water ran out! And if you were on duty late - you were out of luck!

Given our situation, even a simple thing like washing uniforms was a real chore. There were no laundry facilities, or washing machines. The jungle issue uniforms were made of very lightweight ripstop nylon and were easily washed by hand, but they were filthy from our perspiration, dust and dirt after only a few hours. Lacking detergent, we washed them using hand soap, out in the outdoor metal troughs that were also used for washing our faces and brushing our teeth. For a brief period a group of us paid a Vietnamese woman to do our wash but that lasted less than a month. During the summer, the uniforms were dried by hanging them on clothes lines or spreading them out on the revetments until they were dry. During the monsoon season we could get them to dry only if we hung them in our rocket box - they would simply not dry in the air because the humidity was so high. Needless to say the uniforms never got very clean.

When I first arrived, I wondered how anyone slept, all night long there as was outgoing fire from the 175 mm guns, the sound of helicopters taking off and landing, small arms fire from the berm line - and sometimes incoming fire (usually mortars or 122 mm rockets). It was amazing but I soon developed a degree of auditory discrimination both extraordinary and extremely sensitive; it was a sensory perception that allowed me to sleep through the helicopters taking off and landing, the small arms fire from the berm line, the 175s going off- and yet I woke up immediately when incoming fire happened. The mind filtered out the other sounds and let you

A 175mm Gun

81

New Years we embarked on the steamer Iberville and sailed for Baton Rouge to join our Regt. We had a fine passage up and New Years day after we had our tents pitched I hunted up some of the Dexter boys. I saw about all I knew except Charlie Whitmore and Jacob who are sick in the hospital....Two days after we got there our company was sent out on picket duty.... The place where we are stationed is right on the banks of the river....The Secesh and Federals have had several brushes here and perhaps we shall before long and if we do I expect that little will I promoted to Captain for Bravery etc. etc. etc.
One night later:
I have just time to add that we were on picket yesterday and had a small fight with the enemy.... "(Vintage, pgs 134 and 135)

For the next few months, Eugene was on the move. Writing his mother from Opelousas on April 25, 1863:
"Since I wrote last, I have seen some things which look like war. It has been some time since I wrote ....in the afternoon we landed in a place called Indian Bend and marched about two miles...On that march we had to skirmish with the enemy and we lost

sleep - except when it was incoming. If it was incoming, but not hitting our immediate area, we recognized enough difference in the explosions to distinguish between the 122's and the mortars.

While the folding cots kept us off the floor, and while the seahuts were screened in, plenty of mosquitos still got in and so we also slept under mosquito nets. Because malaria was rampant we had to take anti malaria tablets. Two kinds were issued, one you took weekly, a large purple tablet of a chloroquine compound; the other was a small white dapsone tablet you were supposed to take more frequently, but, since the doctor believed the tablets carried more risks than catching that kind of malaria, he advised against taking them.

Additionally we were vaccinated against a number of diseases

A Chinook over the shower house

A view of my hootch

largely unknown in the States such as bubonic plague, yellow fever, polio, and small pox among others. While some of those inoculations lasted for years, others had to be renewed after a few months, and so, among other medical tasks we gave lots and lots of inoculations to the units of the Aviation Group.

Immediately behind our hootch, stretching down a gentle hillside to where a small stream ran, were the remains of an old Vietnamese cemetery. Parts of the firebase were built on other parts of the cemetery. Many of the graves were ornate and although some had been damaged during earlier fighting, most were still standing albeit unkempt and overgrown simply because the Vietnamese families were not allowed on Camp Eagle to tend to them. (I later learned that many Vietnamese believed that it was not a good omen that the American base was built on the grounds of a cemetery and that, because we were desecrating the site, we would suffer accordingly.) It was a haunting place, but one where, on my hours off, I could go to escape the bustle going on around the unit. Visually, it was very interesting: I took some photographs of the graves

several men the next day, ..."
Then he refers to his diary:
"April 24th, we marched about a mile when we saw a smart battle going on in a field before us. Our men were in the field and the Rebels were in line in the edge of the woods...The Rebels had a gunboat the Dianna...and she kept firing shells and shot at us over the Rebels. Our Regt. looked on some time, but at last we got orders to move down the road...As we began to get nearer the woods we heard the bullets whistle and saw the dead and wounded on every hand and it was shocking to see men mangled up as some were. ..
April 20. We reached this place having marched, as General Banks said in his orders about 300 miles in 90 days. This is a deserted place where you cannot get paper, pens or ink.... We have cleared the enemy out of this part of the country and we can now rest." (Vintage, pgs 166 and 167)

A few days later there was another diary entry:

"Tuesday, May 5, 1863. Had drill this afternoon and at 2 this afternoon we packed up and marched and are now pretty tired. Did not camp until long after dark...

Wednesday, May 6. We marched about 20 miles today and are now in camp beside the bayou we have followed all day. I have a touch of sore feet."

For the next ten days his diary records a number of marches of 15 - 20 miles. By the 17th he is at Sims Port on the Atchafalaya River awaiting boats and the means to cross the river. After a couple of days rest the company embarked on transports:

"Friday, May 22, 1863 Last night we arrived Bayou Sarah and disembarked about 12 o'clock. We marched a short distance and then slept about an hour and a half. this morning we have marched about 7 miles to Thompson's Creek. We had some skirmishing on the way and one man wounded. It is showing good.

Sunday, May 24, 1863. About 8 o'clock this morning we got orders to march and we are now laying within a half mile of the enemy's works. We have been shelled and have had some men wounded, including the colonel, slightly,. We are to sleep on our arms tonight...."
(Vintagee, pgs 176 and 178)

He is now at Port Hudson

and even did a couple of sketches.

In time, my corner of Camp Eagle became home and I learned to feel relatively comfortable in my surroundings. I continued to consider myself lucky - even though it was clear that many troops in the larger bases in places like Saigon, Da Nang, or Cam Ranh Bay had air conditioning in both living and working quarters, running hot and cold water, and flush toilets as well other social amenities. It was all relative, and, while in comparison to those places we lived under relatively primitive condition, there were other soldiers in other places who lived under far worse circumstances than we did.

Patrols

Even though the area directly around Eagle was relatively quiet, the countryside and nearby villages were still full of people who had sympathy for the National Liberation Front and contained units of the Viet Cong, operating clandestinely who continued to set ambushes, plant booby traps and conduct raids. While

One of the Vietnamese burial plots

their activity took place mostly at night, and some nighttime ambush patrols were set up by the Americans, most of our patrols were sent out during the day for the purposes of checking the countryside to prevent Viet Cong or NVA units from massing or stockpiling weapons in preparation for attacks. Every unit on Eagle shared in the perimeter security. This meant each unit shared responsibility for manning the berm line at night and was also responsible for the security of a sector of the countryside within a few miles of the berm line. The patrols I went on essentially inspected villages and hamlets, along with the outlying countryside, to ensure that local VC units were not setting up booby traps, ambushes or positioning 122 mm rockets for direct attacks against Eagle. Naturally, every patrol included a medic, and so, on a rotating basis all the medics at the dispensary went out on patrols except for Dave, whose medical skills were needed in the dispensary. So almost every day patrols went out and checked out the perimeter around Camp Eagle. (Night ambush patrols went out on a more irregular basis.)

Since winning the hearts and minds of the people was now part of our mission, the medics who were along on those patrols were there not only as a medical resource to the platoon on patrol, but on a number of occasions we also provided medical support to villagers who would request it. Pacification, now integrated into the division's tactical and strategic objectives as an essential component, meant that we were also attempting to build trust and support among the villagers. While Americans were essentially an occupying force, we tried to behave as if we were not. That meant that sometimes on patrols we often took (or were ordered to take) actions designed to minimize our negative impact on the villagers rather than to maximize our military effectiveness. For example, on some of the patrols I went on, we only gave a cursory glance into homes, shelters and huts, rather than giving each a thorough search. We would also do things like walking in line (an inviting bunched up target) across the dikes between the rice paddies so we would not destroy the rice crops. And, of course, we tried not to disturb the animals and we didn't steal them. So we stayed on the paths and roads and tried, in an all too often patronizing and superficial way, to be good neighbors, conducting civic actions and assisting the Vietnamese. This, of course, was not always the case. Americans in jungle fatigues, wearing flak jackets and helmets, and carrying M-16's, M-60's and M-79's had been commonplace for so many years that they were part of the daily life of the villagers. But we were rarely greeted as friends or liberators And, to me, it was probably exactly this point that symbolized a major weakness in our overall strategy in Vietnam.

When on patrol, I carried my medical bag stuffed with medicines, bandages and other emergency paraphernalia weighing about 25 pounds- and strung a bunch of smoke grenades (of mixed colors) on my pistol belt. (The officer in charge also carried smoke grenades.) Some of the medical supplies I carried were for treatment of the Vietnamese civilians who invariably would come out to meet the patrol and then display a damaged limb or would indicated some other injury or a sickness needing medical attention. The smoke grenades were used for identification purposes. The proper sequence of colors was changed each time you went out so the Viet Cong wouldn't use smoke to confuse support helicopters. While the patrol was always in contact by radio, smoke was used to mark the location of the patrol if you had to call in air support, Cobras or fixed wing aircraft, or if you had to get supporting artillery fire. It also assisted in medical evacuation. If you took a casualty that needed evacuation, you called for a "dustoff" (medical evacuation helicopter). Then when you received a

A farmer's house and field

radio message from the medivac chopper that it was nearby, you popped one colored grenade, the correct one for the day to identify your position, and then another one, when it was judged safe to come in for the casualty. That second color was only identified by the RTO (radio operator) after you popped it, so the pilot would know that you had popped it - not the enemy! The VC had on a number of occasions mimicked that process and had lured helicopters in and then shot them down, so it was important to couple the smoke with voice contact.

The medics went out on patrols on a rotating basis. One of the medics, Jaster - a wonderful, generous guy, (and by his own admission, hyperactive and easily bored) - hated doing most of the tasks in the dispensary, and so he didn't mind going on patrols, for which he would often volunteer, taking the place of another medic. He would also vie with Royce for the medcaps rather than drawing duty in the dispensary. He and Charlie (our Pathfinder medic) also always volunteered for the night ambush patrols. Jaster packed a pistol in addition to his issue M16. This pistol - beat up and rusty - was an old US Government Model 45 Colt, probably dating back to WWII and was "liberated"- meaning it was not issued to him but had been scrounged from somewhere - perhaps even taken from the NVA. When he got ready for a patrol he was a sight: a big lanky guy to begin with decked out with his flak jacket, medical pack, M-16, extra bandoliers of magazines, smoke grenades hanging from his belt along with his trusty old 45 bouncing around on his hip. He looked like an old Ernie Pyle cartoon character. He knew that I was a conscientious objector and that I wouldn't carry an M16 but shortly after he discovered that I was familiar with firearms he began insisting that I pack his .45 whenever I went out on a patrol. He would hand it to me and say; "Don't give me any shit - just take it - use it as a last fucking resort if you must, but take it." And so I began taking the old 45 out on patrols, but, unlike Jaster, I felt foolish having it bang around on my belt and so I stuck it in my medical pack. When he rotated back to the states late in the spring, he gave me the pistol - and later that pistol came close to killing me, but that's a story for a subsequent chapter.

I never wrote home about any specific incidents that happened on my patrols not because I wanted to avoid writing about it, but rather my time on patrols passed by uneventfully. Nothing of a dangerous nature ever happened on any patrol I was on and few patrols in our sector ever encountered any problems during the time I was there. My only references are brief as in a letter to Betsy and Steve (Feb 17) when I say: *"..A patrol today - a nice walk to enjoy. Nothing to report. Kids, adults and water buffalo all peaceful...."* When the patrols were accompanied by ARVN troops there would be occasional arrests of suspected Viet Cong and once, as I recall, there was a discovery of some munitions, but generally it was quiet. Not that things couldn't have happened - things could have easily happened - but, fortunately, they didn't.

Medics on patrol were actively encouraged to provide medical assistance to the Vietnamese villagers when, in the judgment of the commanding officer, it didn't interfere with the safety and effectiveness of the patrol. Some officers would encourage us to provide the medical assistance when it was requested, even though it meant that when the medic was treating the villager, the patrol stopped. Usually that meant the soldiers were to take up defensive positions However they frequently got lazy and bunched up to talk and smoke presenting a tempting target but, again, nothing ever happened. Other officers would not permit those mini "medcaps" and kept the patrol moving, making a reasonable

Entering a village

decision that the safety of the patrol was more important than making friends. Of course, there would sometimes be the sick baby thrust out to you and you would see it was running a high fever, but, given the situation there was little I, or anyone, could do without additional resources. Usually I wasn't able to do even a crude, (let alone complete) examination of the child, and so there was no real hope of discovering the reason for the fever; thus usually all that could be offered was aspirin and the hope that real medical help would be sought and found shortly. It was frustrating to be in that situation - but there was literally nothing more that an individual medic could do.

One particularly scene is etched in my mind: one day as we were returning from a patrol, we noticed a Vietnamese boy of 8 or 9 sitting watching us as we began to go back into Eagle through the berm line. It was suspicious - he was not making threatening gestures, only sitting there passively, but the fact that he was watching us as we began to wend our way back through the elaborately constructed defensive line around Eagle (filled with trip wires, booby traps, and many mines) made the officer in charge nervous. The idea that he could guide some others with hostile intentions through the line later was a thought that occurred to many of us. The lieutenant sent over a couple of soldiers to check him out and they discovered that he had a very badly infected leg wound. It was obvious that he was sitting there hoping that we would notice him and help him with his problem. They called me over and I spent a while cleaning and dressing the wound which was a mess and seemed on the verge of becoming systemic, but since I didn't have any sterile syringes or aqueous penicillin, I couldn't give him an injection that would have knocked it out. I gave him a stiff dose of penicillin pills and then prepared a vial of additional penicillin pills to take for the standard regimen of ten days, but then I discovered that, try as I might, I couldn't give him directions to take the medicine. I tried everything including pantomime, but couldn't get him to show any sign of recognition. My frustration of not being able to converse with him and give him the instructions that he needed to take to cure the infection left me profoundly depressed for the next few days.

We never saw the boy again on subsequent patrols, and I have always wondered what happened to him. (On patrols we tried to change our routes to prevent an ambush being set up. This gave you no chance to see the results of treatment, leaving you only able to wonder what happened to the people you treated.) On medcaps, when we returned to selected villages on a regular basis, we would subsequently see people we had previously

Children outside on a village Medcap

treated and were able to judge the results of our treatments.

The Landscape

Driving toward Hue or Phu Bai, we saw that the teeming shanty towns along the roads were filled with refugees from rural hamlets. The shanty towns were built, almost overnight, largely from scavenged materials. They were occupied by local merchants and entrepreneurs who sold everything that American soldiers might want: whiskey, cigarettes, dope, sex, laundry services. They also provided other services or things the Vietnamese might need such as food, (some of it live, but trussed up for display), bicycles, clothing, housewares, small engine or appliance repair. These little villages, with their open storefront shops, were usually a beehive of activity of all sorts with Vietnamese, soldiers, merchants, farmers, women, children (the youngest ones utterly naked), prostitutes and animals of all types and varieties mixing in a cacophony of sounds and smells. Pigs, chickens, ducks, geese, goats, cows, water buffalo, and dogs mixed with the people. While some animals were trussed up and for sale as food, many animals roamed at will. Water buffalo at that time were the tractors of the rural community and not only pulled the plows in the rice paddies or fields but also pulled the wagons into town loaded with produce, or articles for sale.

The transportation infrastructure of Vietnam was still very primitive at that time - few roads were paved and more often than not there were no real roads. Instead there were rutted dirt (or mud) tracks suitable for water buffalo-drawn wagons. The rural villages or hamlets of the area, were to be found not very far away from the cities. Clusters of simple huts around a few more permanent structures often formed the larger villages. In the case of smaller hamlets, simple huts clustered near each other were often found at the end of a dirt lane surrounded by cultivated fields and rice paddies. In the monsoon season mud was everywhere, and in the dry heat of summer, red dust was thrown up by the passage of any vehicle and coated everyone and everything nearby. Near the coast, there were a number of rivers as well as many small streams and lots of small irrigation canals for the rice paddies.

For many infantry soldiers in Vietnam, a major part of their experience was fighting the land - the water, the foliage, as well as the people who lived there. Because of the helicopter, we often experienced the land differently than did other soldiers who made their way across it rather than over it. While patrols and infantry companies did go out and slog through jungles, they also often were flying over it on the way to an LZ or a firebase. Flying east over the costal terrain of Thua Thien province on missions from Camp Eagle, was to fly over an area of densely populated, largely fertile costal plains, heavily

On patrol - a typical farmer's house

A view of Vin Loc Island

farmed in small plots. Part of the year, flooded rice fields gave the landscape a checkerboard appearance. Looking down at the area, it was possible to get an indication of how intense the war had been in this area. Everywhere there were scars from the war. The fields were grouped around villages or hamlets of a few substantial houses mixed in with very insubstantial structures made of straw or war scrap that had been scrounged and reused - often very creatively. For example while the "tin" (sheet metal) roof panels were ubiquitous, every now and then you would see a roof made from soda and beer cans with their ends cut off , carefully flattened to form roof tiles.

Our Medcaps were largely centered on Vin Loc Island so that was my destination on most helicopter flights. We flew south-east from Eagle. From the air, you noticed all the craters that dotted the landscape - holes left from the intense bombing or shelling. Many of the craters were now filled with water and used as fish ponds. They looked quite benign. But some areas still bore raw scars from recent actions. You also saw the fire support bases with their connecting roads carved out of the landscape like ugly wounds - the red brown of the earth contrasting with the vivid green of the foliage. These were mostly perched on high ground, sometimes very high ground, and it was strange to see the red brown jagged gash carved into the foliage at the top of a brilliantly green hill. Then we passed over the costal bay waters between the mainland and the island where villages would sometimes be clustered together on high ground, or built on stilts over the water with boats tethered to the structures and nets strung across the shallow waters around them.

Flying west toward the A Shau Valley and Laos was another story since the landscape moved from the fertile and densely populated costal plain into increasingly hilly and more sparsely settled lands. The hills were covered by jungle growth, but perched on the tops of many of the hills were the firebases or

Another view of Vin Loc Island and a farmer in the field

lookout posts. The whole area was still scarred from the ongoing war - the intense military actions had moved out there away from Hue during the time immediately preceding my arrival. The area between Eagle and the A Shau was still being contested with continuing hostile encounters although not on the scale of the previous year. I rarely went out toward the A Shau Valley. The one time that I clearly remember was when I was ordered out to Ripcord on short notice because they needed a medic quickly and, since I was on duty, I was delegated. I grabbed my medical bag (which was always packed and ready to go), met the Huey at our landing strip and jumped on along with a stretcher. We flew out, circled for a while and then headed back to Eagle. I was never told what was going on or why I was needed and then not needed; the chopper just landed back at Eagle and the pilot motioned me to get off the Huey.

But, that was in July, and Ripcord was catching a lot of crap at that time and so I can only suppose they had taken casualties that overwhelmed the medics there and felt that an extra medic was needed and then changed their minds. Soon after, the 101st finally pulled out of Ripcord because of overwhelming pressure. (For details about Ripcord, see Keith Nolan's book on Ripcord from Presidio Press.) This level of activity was in sharp contrast to the costal region where the NVA (the North Vietnamese Regular Army) had been largely cleared from the area immediately around Hue and Phu Bai. There, the war consisted mostly of clandestine nighttime ambushes or shelling or small unit actions against the indigenous Viet Cong units still operating.

A view of the hills

Along the coast, the joint efforts at pacification appeared effective and in some ways the tide seemed to be running in favor of the US. While I was there, the official mood was decidedly optimistic - even as many soldiers involved in the actual efforts differed with that assessment.

Chapter 4 Daily routines

Work in the dispensary

When I first arrived, the dispensary was a single seahut about 16 feet wide and 32 feet long. (This was a standard size for these buildings and was based on multiples of a 4 x 8 module - the size of a sheet of plywood.) It was constructed in the same general fashion as were all the other Seahuts with plywood up four feet and then had two feet of screen with canvas flaps which were closed in the monsoon, but it was equipped with better lights, better electrical capabilities and was divided into work areas for the various functions.

Within the dispensary, immediately to the left as you entered, was a mall area with shelves and a counter, (al bulilt from scavenged lumber) that served as the pharmacy and doubled as the records and work area for the medic doing the initial screening of patients . Directly across from that was a small waiting area, immediately beyond that was a general purpose examining room and then beyond that was the doctor's office that doubled as a private examining room, with an adjacent tiny area for a lab. Before the expansion of the facility, our storage area was in our bunker - a large metal shipping container covered with earth and sandbags which also served as an emergency treatment room! After an expansion, we added a separate examining room and doctor's office, made a larger lab area and added a sick bay (separate from the

Roger and Randy in the dispensary

general purpose examining room) along with a better storage area for supplies. As with all sea huts, you could walk down the center of the building but when you got near the walls anyone approaching 6' or over was in danger of banging his head due to the steep pitch of the roof.

In a letter to Betsy and Steve, written in the middle of February 1970 (the last page is dated 17 Feb), I wrote at the top over the salutation :

> *Under separate cover will send you a copy of the Div Newspaper just so you can see what kind of propaganda they feed us!*
>
> *Betsy & Steve;*
>
> *Not too much to report this letter. Things have been very quiet. Tet is over tomorrow and so far it has been quiet on Eagle - elsewhere there have been actions. Firebase Rifle, a few miles from here was hit hard a couple of nights ago (direct hit on the Aid Station & some penetration of the wire - 8 KIA, 12 WIA.) Last night they killed a sapper here on Eagle (on a sector on the other side of camp.)*
>
> *This afternoon (a Sunday) I went out to the wire to watch them blow a couple of barrels of "Fu Gas" a description of which is below. [In the letter I drew a crude diagram .] ..55 gal barrel filled with jellied gasoline & explosives backed by sandbags. It is*

The landscape

put out in front (to one side or the other) of the bunkers along with the Claymores (antipersonnel mines) and is controlled from the bunkers. They were blowing the barrels today in preparation to putting new ones in. [After a while the mixture became unstable] I went out to take a few photos & almost collected a purple heart. They had set up the "Fu Gas" wrong and when it blew - instead of going forward it went up and back (the sandbags were like so much paper.) A few of us were standing on top of the bunker when it blew (taking pictures) - I found my finder filling up with flame & the front of me covered with sand. Needless to say, I went over the back rather quickly. The Fugas was about 30 meters from the bunker (which means it was a hell'uva blast!)

I shall be quite interested in seeing the frame I

Blowing " Fugas"

managed to expose at the moment of the blast.

What I do for entertainment on a Sunday afternoon. (Or the trials and tribulations of being a rear echelon soldier!)

Ah well, there are stranger things. I have a half pound of C-4 (a plastic explosive - looks like putty, explodes like TNT) sitting on my shelf next to my camera. What do I use it for? For heating ; it only explodes if compressed (or set off by a blasting cap) otherwise it burns very well.

17 Feb

A patrol today - a nice walk to enjoy. Nothing to report. Kids, adults and water buffalo all peaceful.

Glad to hear my lens is back. Do I owe you any money?

Hope the loft is beginning to become liveable. (Even if it is expensive, it should be fun watching it develop!)

As you can see - other than the brief incident on Sunday there is nothing to say. It is all a daily routine - very dull.

Andy

A few days later in a letter to my parents I turned to getting news and letters from home:

Feb 21

Letters arrived with my withholding statement just as I was about to ask what had happened to it! Thank you for the book - it was very good. Its now making the rounds of the dispensary.

Speaking of that - in my last letter I had said that Harriet was sending me the "News of the Week" from the Times and that you needn't send it any more - perhaps I shouldn't have said that. It gets passed around & two copies of it won't go to waste. I've told you how much the others (magazines) are appreciated - when everyone is done they get put out in the waiting room where they are devoured.

Also would you send me a slide of my cabin (There ought to be any number of them around!) I've talked about it & now would like to show it . Am returning the pictures of Margie's child & the Phelan tribe. I don't really need them here.

I like the "3 Goldfish" card. [A Christmas card my father made that year.] *(I must say that the holiday season passed here without me even noticing it. I celebrated Tet more than Christmas & New Years!)*

Things are still quiet in the immediate area - however as you have no doubt heard, the Plain of Jars was overrun. What subsequent events that will influence here I don't know.

I really know less of the overall situation than you do!

But I am depressed - as much over what I hear about the States (the Chicago trial - a damned political persecution, Mitchell's statements, etc.) as what is happening here!

Hope Mother & Grandmother got (get?!) off to Alabama. (Sometime I must write Rich Coogan & establish communications before going to DaNang.)....

Andy

Eugene sees action

While his diary entry of May 24, 1863, gives no hint of it, Eugene's life is about to change. Although he was in a few brief skirmishes and participated in the capture of the Saltworks, by and large, the first year of Eugene's time in Louisiana, was spent rather peacefully in garrison duty in New Orleans and the surrounding area,

The ngagements at Irish Bend in April was when he experienced his first real action.

After his diary entry of May 24 (quoted earlier) the entries in the diary outline the intensity of the siege of Port Hudson, Diary entries from the last week of May, 1863 cryptically, but graphically sketch the action:

Monday, May 25, 1863.
We went on picket this morning and have been fighting all along our company. We have lost 1 man killed and 3 wounded. We are in the woods and they creep upon us anywheres. There has been hard fighting on our right.

Tuesday, May 26.

This morning we were relieved and have been in the rear part of the day - fighting still going on.

Wednesday, May 27, 1863.
We are laying near the fort. We charged in it today, but were unable to carry it with the force we had. Our company, or part of it, were just on the ramparts. We lost this time 2 killed and 5 wounded. One man was shot at my side when we just charged up to the works. We had a hard fight of it."
(Vintage, pgs 1.78 - 179)

Thursday, May 28, 1863

We fell back this morning and have been laying in the woods. Fighting is stilled for the present on account of a flag of truce to bury the dead. It is to commence again at 7 o'clock tonight, however.

Friday,, May 29.
We were called out last night to support a Battery. We were under fire, but lost no men in our company. However fighting is still going on fiercely.

The Plain of Jars was in Laos, and this note referred to the fact that it had fallen to the Communist Pathet Lao. The reference to the Chicago Trial was a reference to the prosecution and trial of members of a Vietnam War protest group who had disrupted the Democratic Convention the previous summer and thus had embarrassed the then Mayor of Chicago, Richard Daley. He vigorously pressed for severe penalties for the protestors, and the resulting trial of the Chicago Seven, as they were referred to, was conducted in a circus-like atmosphere that made national headlines. While two defendants were acquitted, the others were found guilty and sentenced to long prison sentences. On appeal in 1972, they were all acquitted of the most serious conspiracy charges.

By the middle of February, things had settled into something of a routine. The medics at the dispensary got along very well most of the time. Both Dave and the Captain were medical professionals before they were soldiers and so our routines within the dispensary were more established along the lines of medical protocol rather than being based on Army regulations. (Outside the dispensary, of course, it was all Army!) The other medics Jim, Bruce, Roger, Randy, Royce and Charlie were all capable, responsible and did what needed to be done. Everyone had to know various parts of the operation in the running of the dispensary so as to cover when people went out on patrols, off to do special jobs or were doing Medcaps. We all shared a number of duties. During the first few months I was there, I participated in all procedures and did all the things that were part of our responsibilities in order to learn about the operations of the dispensary. However, because of the interests and skills of each of us, Dave and Capt. (Dr.) M gave each medic primary areas of responsibility. If someone wanted to learn more about certain areas or procedures, he was encouraged to do so if he showed any aptitude for the task. As a result, my memories are that we effectively "meshed" as a unit and built a very cohesive working relationship that endured for many months.

When I first arrived, Royce was maintaining the pharmacy and also going out on Medcaps very frequently. As I learned more and more about pharmacology, and since I displayed a talent for asking soldiers entering on sick call key questions about their symptoms, I was increasingly given the responsibility for managing the admittance of daily sick call, as well as more and more of the responsibility for the pharmacy. After a couple of months, both the screening of sick call patients and the pharmacy became my primary areas of responsibility. Royce, far from being distressed about an exchange of roles, was delighted to spend more and more of his time flying or on Medcaps. I liked learning about symptoms, and about drug usage, effectiveness, and interactions as well as contra-indications, and so I eagerly studied the Physicians Desk reference and the Pharmacology references, as well as picked Dave's and Capt. M's brains as much as I could. And, in a relatively short time, I developed some real skills in diagnosing and treating illnesses.

I also discovered a talent for dealing with trauma wounds, an area that some of the others were not fond of, but one which I found myself enjoying. I didn't mind debriding (cutting away damaged tissue) and I really enjoyed the suturing. Perhaps it was the artist in me that enjoyed the artistry in the precise wielding of scalpel, needle and thread. I was attracted by the skill it took to cut off damaged tissue or to pull two edges of flesh together, insert the needle and thread and tie an effective knot folding the edges neatly together. The medics did a lot of suturing in the dispensary - even when the doctor was there and on duty. There was such a great need for it that once

Saturday, May 31.

Last night we went on picket and are now laying before the works. I do not know as we have lost any men yet. (Vintage, pg. 183)

He wrote a long letter home on June 1, but did not give any details about this action, although he says:: "*...have had some hard fighting, but I think it is about over with, now,...Our Regt. has been in some hard places but we are now in a comparatively safe place...*" (Vintage, pg. 185) It was only in September when, after his father saw the diary entries quoted above, that Eugene wrioe home in any detail about the action. (Eugene mailed home his diaries every so often.) In the September letter, Eugene goes into great detail (as he remembers it) of his activities during the three days commencing on the 24th - complete with a great deal of heroic description.

However, in that June 1, letter he wrote :

... I have not had a chance to write before as I should, because I know you must have felt anxious but God has preserved me so far and I feel almost sure that he will see me through

safe. We have lost some men from our company but none you know. Mell [Gould] is first rate and so am I. I do not want you to feel at all alarmed if you do not receive another letter for some time for it is a hard sight for a fellow to write here. Tell Charley that I think I knocked over one Sesech in good shape and shall do the same by another if I get a good chance. Mell and I were two of the first in the ditch when we charged the works a few days ago and we have the name of being pretty plucky boys. You will see accounts of our proceedings in the paper, I suppose so that it will be useless for me to write home on what I am not properly posted on....
(Vintage, pgs 1.84-185)

He iwas referring to the first unsuccessful attempt to storm Port Hudson. After falling back and regrouping,
by June 12 Eugene's company was making preparations to join another storming party. His diary notes the preparations in a very matter of fact manner:

"Saturday, June 13. We have received orders to be ready to join the storming party tonight and we have been getting cartridges and preparing

we had been trained we handled a lot of it and while it became routine, it always remained challenging.

Sometimes the challenges became a panacea for overcoming boredom. One afternoon, when I was off duty and had been relaxing at the hootch reading, napping and drinking warm beer (having pulled night duty the evening before) I became bored, and so I wandered up to the dispensary just to see what was going on. I managed to walk in just as they were admitting a soldier with an interesting trauma wound that required extensive suturing. I don't remember what the wound was - but I do remember that it was serious though not life threatening and it looked very interesting and quite challenging. So interesting in fact, that I offered to flip a coin with whoever was working on it for the rights to finish the treatment, *i.e.* to do the suturing - and I won the coin toss. (The soldier being treated didn't know what to make of that but he was worried. It wasn't until about ten days later when we removed the sutures that he relaxed - the wound had healed very well.)

That was one of the saving things about my duty - it was interesting to learn about medicine and medical procedures. I think in the long run that helped to keep me focused. Even in the midst of an awful war, you could - legitimately - feel like you were doing something positive. You were helping to heal people or helping people recover. We didn't see a lot of terrible trauma from bullet wounds (the soldiers wounded that badly went directly by medivac helicopter to the 325th Field Surgical Hospital), but frequently we did see shrapnel wounds along with fractures, burns (a few very bad ones) and all sorts of infections and skin problems. On Medcaps, you would see all sorts of problems with the Vietnamese, but we could only treat the infections and simple problems. If they were suffering from more serious problems we referred them to hospitals when we could get the clearance to do so. But even modest help made a difference. You would clean the wound, give antibiotics and then a week later, they would be much improved or even symptom free. You felt good about that.

The Working Routine

I described my situation and daily activities in a letter, dated on March 12, 1970 to Sue and Bob Turner (family friends):

Speaking of my work (I don't know how much you know so I shall tell you briefly), I work in an Aviation Unit dispensary. Mainly we handle sick call and perform flight physicals - however we are a brigade level unit so we co-ordinate most of the flight physicals in the division. While most of the medical work is routine I have learned a great deal. The working hours are regular - except we work a 7 day week - and we generally get a morning and an afternoon off....

Inside the dispensary

for hot work generally.

Sunday, the 14th. Last night about 12 we got into line and today we have been fighting like fury. Our loss is very heavy and yet we have failed to carry the works. I was hit by a spent shell which lamed my hand and I had to cease firing. I shot one Rebel I think." (Vintage, pg 1.87)

Monday, June 15. We have been laying before the Rebel works all day firing and taking what comes from the other side also. The loss in our company yesterday was one killed and two wounded

Tuesday, June 16. I was on guard last night up to our breast works which have been building. We manage to get our meals regular which is a blessing.

Wednesday, 17. In the same place occasionally firing at a Rebel. Our breast works are going on finely and we are extending them every night.. (Vintage, pg 188)

After that they settled in for a lengthy siege, sheltered by breastworks and trenches. I visited Port Hudson a,nd those trenches and breastworks that Eugene mentions were about 30 yards from, and below, the Confederate fortifications. It was a very exposed position to say the least. It seems that for all soldiers, the mind gradually but inevitably accepts the hazards of the job as normal. The constant threat of death and destruction is placed in the context of "normalcy"! Here are some of his subsequent diary entries when his company was occupying those front trenches which kept them engaged in sniping and harassing activity - and being sniped at in return - sometimes with fatal results:

"Thursday, June 18, 1863 We had one man from our company wounded today. We occupy our time reading and playing checkers.

Friday 19   Nothing unusual today excepting one man killed and 3 wounded in our Regt. The one killed belonged to Company B.

Saturday 20 Last night we went and relieved the 52nd Mass. which have gone out with a wagon train. We are in rather a hard place and can only go out by night without being greatly exposed."
(Vintage, pg. 189)

Our days began early. I usually awoke before dawn (I don't remember what time they sounded reveille.) It was a nice time - as cool as the day would get and still peaceful. After breakfast, I would try to get to the dispensary early, usually shortly after 7 AM, so I would have a few minutes before everyone else came on duty. I would brew a pot of coffee and enjoy a cup while I arranged things for the day. Sick call started about 8 AM and there were days when we had people lined up outside the dispensary awaiting the hour. The problems were many and varied.

Both GIs and the Vietnamese who were authorized to be on base would show up with various ailments. Some were sick with the flu, or with dysentery, or with a variety of other problems from trench foot gone bad, to insect bites that had become infected, to venereal infections from god knows where. We took each and every person who came through the door. We took people on a first come basis - except for emergencies. Mostly patients were soldiers but sometimes they were Vietnamese civilians working on the base or ARVN troops on temporary duty with the Pathfinder unit. With most of the problems we were able to make a diagnosis and prescribed treatment, but with some we had to refer them to the 326th Medical Battalion Hospital for more extensive treatment. After lunch, we normally attended to the ongoing business of the dispensary, giving flight physicals or conducting group inoculations, often on site at the other units of the Aviation Group. I got so proficient at giving inoculations that I would often give them two at a time - placing two syringes between the fingers of one hand and poking them in the arm simultaneously. However, the afternoons were also when we would see the casualties after the troops got back from operations. Then we would see shrapnel or minor bullet wounds or lacerations.

Randy and Jim

Normal duty days lasted until 5 or 6 PM and then, unless one had the night duty in the dispensary, we were free to relax in the hootch talking, writing letters, reading, listening to the radio, washing clothes, mending equipment, etc. Sometimes we went to the EM's club (enlisted men's club) - a fancy name for what was, in reality, a hootch with tables where they sold

His diary comments are at odds with his letters home. In a letter to his brother written, as he put it, "Before Port Hudson" and dated June 29 he comments:

"Our last charge was an unsuccessful one, and we lost a large number of men but kept our ground and erected breast works which now protect us...", and then after saying that, goes on to say : *...We have breast works erected now within a hundred feet of the enemy and the next attempt must prove successful. We are having pretty hard times now, but not from the enemy's fire but from the hotter rays of old Sol....We are pestered with mosquitoes by night and flies by day, making it almost impossible to get any sleep....I enjoy excellent health and I believe the hotter the weather the better I feel. We have some good times if the bullets do whistle down behind our earth works. We play checkers and read the papers in almost perfect safety. You need not feel anxious about me for we have a fine place here excepting the sun... If I had a chance to send home things I would send a few little trinkets I have picked up in the shape of 32lb. shells and old muskets...."*

109

(Vintage, pgs. 190 and 191)

In that same letter, he also reveals that he has been considerably sobered by his participation in the unsuccessful storming, but remains committed to do his duty:

"...Our last charge was an unsuccessful one, and we lost a large number of men but kept our ground and erected breast works which now protect us. The next storming party is to be formed of volunteers, and I should have volunteered but I thought that you would rather I do my duty with my company and not volunteer to go into great danger for a name. When the Regt. or company goes, I shall go with it and my officers have given me the praise of being a brave fellow..."
(Vintage, pg. 191)

Tuesday, July 7. Heard that Vicksburg was taken. Great cheering and rejoicing over it. Brisk cannonading our company came off fatigue this morning.

Wednesday 8. Port Hudson has surrendered to General Banks. Firing has ceased. I can hardly recognize it as yet, the stillness is something uncommon....

(expensive) warm beer or soda, played loud music and provided bare tables where you could sit and talk with others. That was the only place where you socially met others who had different duty assignments.

During the monsoon months we spent largely dreary evenings inside the medics' hootch sheltered against the incessant cold rains. We listened to the rain beat down on the tin roofs while we read, listened to music, or wrote letters. During the summer, we would sit out behind the hootch drinking sodas or beers while quietly talking or listening to music, while those who smoked did so. We had a view of the berm line and would watch the periodic outgoing fire. Summer evenings were, relatively speaking, pleasant reprieves from the heat of the day, although during the summer months it remained very hot in the evening - indeed it remained hot all night long. We slept under mosquito netting with our fans on us! Evenings were never quiet, choppers were always in the air and the evening interdiction fire from the 175s frequently started shortly after dark. The berm line always seemed to have some activity going on not long after it got dark - normally that early in the evening it was in response to imagined enemy activity. The real action usually started long after midnight.

We were excused from guard duty on the berm line, but in place of that we pulled night duty in the dispensary. One medic was on duty in the dispensary every night. Rotation depended on how many of the medics were available - often we were at less than full strength since, for example, at any given time someone might be on an R & R or on an assignment out of camp. We always had someone on duty so there were a few times when we went for a couple of weeks pulling duty every third night but normally it was more likely every 4-5 nights.

The Perfume River

After Captain M left in April, following a medical emergency regarding his wife, we were without a doctor for about a month and a half. The new doctor, Capt. R, arrived in June but during the interim we carried on with the help of a visiting doctor from another aviation unit who spent a few hours a week at the dispensary doing the flight physicals.

Pacification and Medcaps

The idea of pacification meant that the Division helped the Vietnamese local populace with projects such as building roads, water purification or sanitation projects, helping build facilities like schools, or improving medical services. To the East of the city of Hue was Vin Loc, a very large and fertile island, stretching north and south along the coast. It had long been a stronghold of the VC. Many of our division's pacification efforts were done in the area immediately around Hue, but our unit's efforts were centered on this island, where, because of our airmobility, we could deliver personnel to remote villages by helicopter to assist in all the civic actions which included medcaps.

Thursday, July 9, 1863. We marched into the fort this morning and were received by the Rebels in a line of battle....and they grounded arms.

(Vintage, pg. 194)

There was no time to savor the victory, on Saturday the 11th, his diary entry reads: *This forenoon about 11 o'clock we embarked on the Laurel Hill down river. I am quite unwell today. It has been raining pretty hard this afternoon. It is night and we have passed Baton Rouge. How much further to go I do not know but we land at Donaldsonville I think.*

He then wrote his brother from Donaldsonville:

  "I was in hopes to date my next letter in Port Hudson but we did not stop long enough in the place to look around. Port Hudson surrendered on the 8th and our troops marched in on the morning of the 9th. Our Regt. was one of the first to enter and it did me good to seethe long lines of battle units drawn up with arms grounded and prisoners of war..
(Vintage, pgs. 197 and 198)

111

The Viet Cong had successfully followed the Maoist model of guerrilla war in which they not only waged a literal war against the government in Saigon, but on a local level they also sought to replace the designated officials with their own governmental structure. The success of this strategy had become clear to political leaders in the United States who realized that we would never extricate ourselves from the war as long as the government of Vietnam lacked legitimacy. These medical missions grew out of the rather belated American understanding of the need to coordinate the building of support for the government in Saigon with the military effort. While there had been sporadic efforts at pacification starting as early as 1959 under the Agroville program, they were abandoned a year later but then reincarnated in 1961 as the Strategic Hamlet program. This also was neglected as the government faced a number of crises in 1963 in the major population centers ceding the countryside to the Viet Cong. In 1968, recognizing the ongoing failure of the Saigon government to effectively handle the

Waiting for the medics

Vietnamese medical personnel on a joint Medcap

responsibility for the pacification campaign, that program was shifted to fall under the direct responsibility of MACV. As part of those pacification efforts the 101st began an extensive civil actions campaign in the province (Thui Thien) and integral to that effort were the Medcaps. Medcaps were small groups of medical action teams that went out into the villages and rural areas providing medical assistance to the Vietnamese civilian population. They also involved teaching the Vietnamese some basic medical skills. An article in the Division newspaper, *The Screaming Eagle*, on Feb 16, 1970 featured an article on the effort and ended as follows: *"..The ultimate goal of the program... is to develop a skilled Vietnamese medical cadre who can carry on the teaching program independent of the Screaming Eagles."* (Vol III, No 5, pg. 8 columns 1-3)

Our dispensary was heavily involved in this part of the pacification effort. We usually scheduled one or two Medcaps a week, weather permitting. One -occasionally two - medics from the Aviation Group dispensary, along with ARVN troops and medical personnel (trained personnel were rare) and a few ARVN and 101st Airborne infantrymen for protection, would be flown out in helicopters to a village. A medical clinic would be set up for the day and would treat the villagers for a variety of ailments. We would be picked up at the end of the day. A few days to a week later, the team would return to conduct a follow-up visit. (The follow-up was on a random schedule so as to avoid an ambush. While VC ambushes had become increasingly rare by 1970, they were still possible and occasionally happened, so we took precautions not to become too complacent about the Medcaps.) The NVA and VC tried hard to prevent the Saigon based government from delivering essential services - including medical services - as part of their strategy of portraying the government as inept and uncaring.

When we arrived at a location, lines would form outside the site of the medical action team's location, and there was frequently a good deal of initial jostling to be first in line. The ARVN and American infantry would set up a line, get it into some semblance of order and then admit patients for a kind of sorting or

Another view of the Medcap on Vin Loc Island

triage screening in as orderly a fashion as possible. Weeping mothers with very sick infants or people with obviously serious injuries, or who were extremely sick, were admitted first. Those with less serious injuries would end up waiting for much of the day to be examined by an American medic. (Doctors did not normally go along on the Medcaps so the primary medical assistance was done by the medics.)

The villagers would crowd around us during the visit. Usually we had to hold the visit in some place where we could control the access so we would not be overwhelmed. Frequently (as shown in the photographs) that location was in a school or church. ARVN troops were set up to try to control the crowds and access to the examining area. Sometimes it worked - sometimes it didn't.

Most of the medical problems we saw and treated were from sickness, infections or accidents. Occasionally, we saw the results of booby traps or mines. The climate - warm and moist - made for a very fertile atmosphere that nurtured germs, and the use of "night soil" (human excrement) as fertilizer enhanced the potential for the spread of diseases. Sanitation problems and the fact that most Vietnamese were living under very primitive conditions, including the duress of war, further exacerbated existing problems. We gave tons of inoculations, cleaned out infected wounds, bandaged lacerations, applied topical fungicides and gave lots of injections of antibiotics for the huge number of serious infections we saw. Children were some of our most frequent patients. Giving babies huge shots of penicillin (1500 cc's - three times the stateside standard) for infections made me cringe every time I plunged that huge needle into their tiny buttocks. But that level of dosage was needed to combat the increasingly drug resistant diseases and infectious agents that were present in Vietnam. Unfortunately, when we saw serious diseases that required extended or complex treatment, we could only recommend that the person be taken to a hospital. Sadly, those needing extensive attention were rarely able to gain access to the treatment since medical facilities were few and far between. For the average Vietnamese villager, they were largely inaccessible.

Ross particularly enjoyed going on medcaps and he spent much of his time on them . Small, wiry and very soft spoken, he was a deeply religious conscientious objector who brought a missionary zeal to this work. He often described his work on the medcaps in the same way that missionaries might describe their work among the unconverted. He was an excellent person for these missions, believing deeply in the need and reacting with true feelings for the people he treated. (Somewhat incongruously, to my mind, when Ross rotated back to the states at the end of his term of service, he bequeathed to me a large and very sharp hunting knife that he always carried. He kept it polished and sharpened to a razor edge.) After Ross left, Bruce took over many of his tasks with much the same missionary zeal - but with a more dogmatically righteous conviction, believing as he always did, that his appointed mission and that of the U.S. Army was as a savior to the Vietnamese people.

Medcaps were very emotionally satisfying events for me, but physically very draining since they lasted all day with a short lunch break. You were busy almost all the time, operating with intense concentration in very primitive conditions while confronting many different aliments in the space of a few hours even as you frequently coped with some notable degree of chaos. You almost always examined patients in front of an audience who watched your every move intently, either crowding into the room or looking in the windows. The audience would collectively wince or cry out when a boil was lanced, a wound sutured, or an injection given. And sometimes they would cheer when a patient was treated with immediately obvious positive results. Sometimes, if we weren't sure of a diagnosis, we would bring back specimens of blood or urine, and run lab tests at the dispensary. For more sophisticated analyses than possible in our rudimentary lab, we would send the specimens to the 326th medical lab connected with the division's field hospital. Treatment would then be administered whenever we went back to the same village on a subsequent medcap - usually within a couple of weeks. It was always nice to return to a village and see the results - often dramatic - of treatment you were able to give.

My limited duty as a Muralist

I did some drawing while in the Army, but very few drawings in Vietnam. I only sent home one illustrated letter - and that wasn't much of an illustration. Only a few of my sketches survive and those have been reproduced in this book.. But one very interesting experience happened as a result of my drawing early in my tour at Eagle. The Aviation Group Sergeant Major found me sketching one day when I was off duty and relaxing. When he came over I leaped to my feet and stood at attention - very nervous. I had learned very early in my Army career, that you did nothing that would emphasize your own uniqueness - and certainly not about things creative - lest you draw the wrath of a sergeant or officer. He asked me what I was doing. When I told him, much to my surprise, instead of chewing me out, he asked if he could see my sketch book. Quite worried, I reluctantly gave it to him and after looking at it intently, he asked me if I would take on a project for him. I answered in the

Eugene Kingman, the Illustrator

One of the things that fascinated me about Eugene was that , particularly early in his service, he sent home lots of illustrated letters and a number of drawings.

Photographs of course, existed, as the haunting photographs of Matthew Brady and others remind us, but those cameras, which used glass plates and were large and bulky were not something that soldiers carried with them as soldiers a century later did in Vietnam, and so it was natural for those who could sketch and draw to send home sketches of the war. Those who did not draw frequently asked those who did to do drawings for them to include with their letters. For example Eugene comments in many letters how he was asked to do drawings for others.

In a letter dated December 8, 1861, from Camp Chase (Lowell, Mass.) where he was stationed during his training, he wrote:

"...I do not get much time to sketch and draw, but I do some and have sold some pictures and have got paper

affirmative, since a Specialist 4 didn't refuse the request of a sergeant major under any circumstances. He then proceeded to explain to me that he wanted a mural done in the mess hall and he said that if I would be willing to consider the task, he would have me relieved from my regular duty while I was working on it.

We went and looked at the wall in the mess hall. It was a big wall - about 25 feet long, and I indicated that while I was interested, not only was it a big job but I didn't have any of the proper tools - such as oil paint or artists brushes suitable for a mural. So I wasn't certain I could complete the job and said so. Not a problem he assured me - "just let me know what you want in the way of brushes and paint, and I'll get it for you." I gave him a list thinking that would be the end of it, but a couple of weeks later he came to the dispensary looking for me with the paints and brushes I ordered. He then arranged for me to be relieved of my regular duties for a week in return for the assignment to paint the mural in the mess hall. When I begin to plan it, he asked me to make sketches based on a scene that he had in mind. What he wanted was an action scene of 101st Airborne infantry being inserted into a landing zone by helicopters. I prepared the sketches and while, in general, he liked them he had something else in mind and said as much.

To my surprise - he wanted the mural done as a low relief diorama. He wanted me to include models of Hueys and Chinooks in the picture. I agreed that it was an interesting idea, but asked where I would get models of the helicopters? "No problem," he replied - "I already have them - I ordered them from the same hobby shop in Japan when I ordered your paint and brushes - I hoped you might agree with my idea." A week later - after long days painting - I had completed (under his constant, watchful eyes and critical comments that ensured the accuracy of the scene) an 8 x 15 foot long mural portraying swooping Hueys and Chinooks, high grass dramatically billowing under the rotor wash, lifting off after a hot insertion of 101st Airborne Infantry. Overhead several Cobras provided suppression fire against a nearby tree line. He was very pleased and proud of that mural. For about 48 hours I basked in the appreciation of the mural - getting congratulations from a number of my fellow soldiers - and then I returned to my anonymous role as a medic. But the mural cemented my relationship with the Sergeant Major, but also (and equally importantly) with the cooks, and for the rest of my tour they treated me with special attention.

Guns for Stethoscopes

While in Vietnam, I watched (or heard) how other determined men found creative and constructive ways to improvise unorthodox solutions or get around the rigidity of the Army's support and supply structure in order to accomplish something that they felt improved the situation. A wonderfully illustrative case in point involved the expansion of the 101st Aviation Group Dispensary not long after I arrived there. Not only did it circumvent the limitations of the Army's unresponsive bureaucracy, but it also involved some modern alchemy- which turned captured enemy guns into improved medical facilities.

The expansion of the 101st Aviation Group dispensary was requested when it became clear to Dr. M that the dispensary was not large enough to properly handle all the responsibilities, activities and demands placed on it by the units it supported, and additionally was simply not able to handle the volume of flight physicals the division required. There were many days when we had an extended line out the door and additional

and envelopes to pay for it. here is a plan of our encampment which shows how we are situated...."
(Vintage, pg. 23)

The previously quoted letter from Fort Monroe, in January 1862 twas another example as is the following from Ship Island in April where he includes two sketches and refers to a request from the Captain for another:

"...Here is a plan for the island (details also listed) It is much longer in proportion than I have represented it here but it will give you some idea of how we are campcamped. Our camp ground is all sand and just as white as snow...
...I just saw. the Captain and he wanted me to take a sketch of one of the steamers we took from the Rebels and he said he would send it on to Harper's Weekly and I guess I shall do it.....
...Here is a sketch of a Zouave for Alice..."
(Vintage, pgs. 62 and 63)

The "commissions", for that is what they were, probably started Eugene on his subsequent career as illustrator.

119

people waiting to get in for flight physicals or for problems which often needed immediate attention. A flight physical would be conducted in the corner of the sick bay/examining room (one and the same) adjacent to a patient undergoing treatment. In addition, sick soldiers had to be sent back to their hootches because we didn't have a sufficient sick bay where we could keep them under observation. The routine lab work had to be shipped out to the 326th because we didn't have a microscope or other rudimentary pieces of equipment - we could get them, but even if we had them, there was no place to set them up. The inevitable delay meant that completion of the flight physical was delayed until the lab work was returned.

I don't know exactly when the expansion proposal for the enlargement of the dispensary had been submitted, but probably it was either in December '69 or in January '70, nor do I know where it had to go for approval, I do know that a formal request was submitted and disappeared into the bureaucracy of the Division. Nothing happened for several months, and in the interim the situation grew increasingly desperate as the demands multiplied and the number of people we saw daily continued to increase. So Capt. M, impatient and chaffing at the delay, decided to do something about it and devised a plan to procure the necessary materials unofficially. The way it was accomplished tells a lot about how any number of things got accomplished in the Army - particularly in Vietnam

The author (looking very spiffy!)

- when the official channels proved unresponsive or too cumbersome. Although having said that - I suspect that in peacetime the bureaucracy would win!

The Captain secured the cooperation of a number of other officers in the Aviation Group, including the Pathfinders and the transportation unit as well as the commander of the Group. He first asked the Pathfinders to give up some of their captured NVA or Viet Cong weapons, which they did very willingly. These weapons consisted largely of a motley collection of older SKS rifles, some even older Carl Gustav (Swedish) submachine guns but included a few highly prized AK47's. All of these weapons were coveted by American GI's as war trophies and some of them - but not all - could legally be taken home as certified war trophies. Then he rounded up some two and a half ton trucks and a few volunteer drivers and proceeded to set up a convoy that went down to DaNang. In DaNang, one of the major ports, where supplies were unloaded and stored for distribution to all the military units in I Corps, he made contact with some of the Navy Seabee units and proceeded to trade the war trophy guns for the necessary (but unauthorized) building materials (plywood, 2 x 4's and tin roofing material) and then transported them back up to Camp Eagle where we proceeded to build an unauthorized, but certainly a much needed addition to the dispensary.

It was while we were preparing the guns for trade that the other medics discovered something about me which came as a shock to them. They found out that I knew quite a lot about weapons. They were trying to figure out how to dissemble some of the weapons (the SKS's, AK 47's and Swedish Carl Gustav subma-chine guns) for cleaning and were having little success with it, until, to their astonishment, I showed them how to break down both the AK 47 and the Carl Gustav. So it became a running joke around the dispensary that I was their resident weapons expert disguised as a conscientious objector.

After the building materials acquired in the trade arrived, we began the construction. Very quickly the dispensary was doubled in size by adding a parallel seahut, and a connecting passageway between the two buildings provided a structure shaped like an H. This enabled us to set up a larger examining area and an office/examining room for the doctor who desperately needed that space, not only because of the demand for a private examining room but also for the inevitable paperwork. We were also able to set up and equip a small lab and set aside space for a temporary sick bay where we could keep patients who needed supervised attention but were not sick enough to warrant sending on to the 326th Medical Battalion Hospital.

The new addition was an immediate success. To see something develop by circumventing wartime bureaucracy was interesting to say the least. To see the building completed -even though you knew it was a temporary structure - gave you something constructive to point to , rather than something destructive to lament. The building was a temporary structure by virtue of the materials used and the transitory nature of war, but this did not diminish the sense of accomplishment.

The first 122's hit on My Watch

March 20

Betsy & Steve,

We got hit -hard- with rockets a week ago. 12-14 of them fell in the Group area - all of them within 100 yards of the dispensary where I happened to be on duty (4 am in the morning!) Took two direct hits on hootches but by some freak everyone had gotten clear (into bunkers) so we had only cuts and bruises, no serious injuries. We also had some shrapnel in vehicles & one Chinook (helicopter) was wrecked. We were lucky.

Fire bases are getting hit very close by so perhaps its going to be a very hot summer. There is a lot of action in I Corp right now. I sleep lightly - those rockets are no joke! Needless to say when they came in I hit the bunker - pronto! And it didn't seem any too thick. (You couldn't do a damn thing except hope nothing landed on you!)....

Then I went on to other things of equal interest:

We are adding on to the dispensary now so things are in a state of confusion around here.

Your loft sounds good - got a letter from Doug Sassi after he had been there and he loved it. In fact as he probably told you, he wants one. (Even asked me if I were interested in sharing one!)

I hope you have hot water by now. (Even I have that twice or 3 times a week!)

Finally got another Canon (with a f1.2 lens) so now I'll be able to start taking some more pictures when I get a chance to get off this place!

Got a letter from Susanjean telling me of her visit with you and Judy & how she enjoyed it!

Susan Platt is back in NYC & asked for your tel number. I gave her your address & told her to try your old number first (I have no idea whether you kept the same tel number.) Anyhow she is working as a secretary (somewhere) & planning to go back to grad school.

I haven't heard from Harriet for a month or so - not really unusual - but am curious if you have heard from her?

Sean wrote me that he got very good grades. A couple of B's & 3C's if I remember correctly. Also it sounds like he is really enjoying himself. Beginning to anyway.

About the time you get this letter (if the mailmen still are on strike) April 5 will mark the 1/3 point of my 1 yr tour. (I may extend in order to get out of the Army early.)

You should be starting to see the first signs of Spring about now? Yes. New York should be very nice the next few weeks.

Andy

In reading these letters 30 years later I am struck by how I was careful about what I said and was consciously trying to play down the drama. I usually mixed in the scary news with much more mundane events - which was the way life was then! But, I can see I was still filled with a little bravado as indicated by my mention of extending. In the letters I was not consistent as to the number of rockets that actually hit the Aviation Group but it really doesn't matter - there were plenty of them, and while a couple were duds - most weren't . They bracketed the dispensary where I was on duty and it seemed to me that they were using the dispensary as the aiming point. That night, I was made aware of how vulnerable one was - and how much luck was a factor in whether one lived or died. Had the aiming sticks been moved an inch or two, rockets could easily have landed directly on the dispensary. It's also fascinating to realize how much I was focused on events back in the world.

This particular attack made its way into a small article in the New York Times - which my parents clipped and sent me. So I wrote back to them:

> *March 24*
>
> *Hi*
>
> *Got your letter in spite of the postal strike. How soon you will get this is a matter of conjecture.*
> *That clipping from the Times - I can tell you all about those rockets because 8-10 of them (two were duds) hit within 100 yards of the dispensary (a couple very close) where I happened to be on duty (at 4:30 AM). Needless to say, I hit the bunker pronto. And stayed there. Scared. We have a very good bunker but that time it didn't feel strong enough! The rockets hit two hootches & a helicopter - but everyone was clear (in bunkers) by some fluke - very lucky.*
> *Needless to say I haven't slept very heavily the last week!...*

Then, as the rocket attack was part of the daily routine I went on (in the letter) to other things, some very mundane, as I had in my letter to my sister:

> *We are building on the dispensary here so things are hectic - which is both good and bad. Good that it breaks the monotony & gives me something interestingly different to do; bad in that our normal operations are greatly hampered.*
>
> *Will send some money on to help pay for the car. It probably shouldn't have been fixed but since it has been & for that price I shall keep it & get another year or two out of it.*
>
> *Books arrived from Mr. Clicquennois & from Mrs. Randolph. Please pass my "Thank you" on. They - the books- are well received. (I put Mr. C's out in the waiting room & they were all gone in 3 days!)*
>
> *I am not doing too much reading now...*

Rereading my letters I'm still struck by how much I toned down the severity of this attack in my letter to my parents (as well as to Betsy and Steve). That particular attack was typically effective - subsequent attacks would be equally effective in causing damage to facilities and to helicopters but they caused relatively few serious casualties among the troops on Eagle.

Rocket attacks almost always occurred at night - usually about 3 or 4 AM. These night attacks occurred largely because security in the immediate area was pretty good and our control of the air gave us surveillance capabilities that generally allowed us to detect any daylight attack - or if we didn't detect them ahead of time, daylight gave us a tremendous advantage to blunt the attack by calling close support airpower - unless the weather was so bad it prevented it! Night attacks gave the VC or NVA the cover of darkness to set up - and then escape.

Since many of the 122's seemed to have been aimed specifically at the dispensary, that night remains very vivid to me. I recall that I was sitting in a chair dozing when the first rocket hit - very close to the dispensary - without my hearing it come in. It burst with a terrific roar and splattered the roof with shrapnel The next few 122's hit a bit more distant to the dispensary. But, after the first one, I went into the bunker as fast as I could and lay down while the ground shook as the rockets began slamming into the ground nearer and nearer. They seemed to be walking back towards me. The last few times, the rockets were close enough that the explosions sent showers of shrapnel and debris rattling on the tin roof of the dispensary. By then I was trying to make my body fuse into the ground and the bunker did not seem nearly strong enough. It was all over in about 20 minutes. And then we were busy with casualties (all minor) for the next two hours.

The 122 mm rockets, used with great success by the Viet Cong or NVA, were easy to set up since frequently they were aimed and launched with the aid of simple wooden aiming sticks. They broke into two pieces (the rocket and the launcher tube) and they were also quite portable and had a fairly good range - almost 11,000 meters. Once they reached their predetermined launch destination point the assembly and launch could be effected in a very short time. These attributes allowed the 122's to be set up in preselected locations at night far enough away from the target so as to generally avoid detection. They also carried a large enough explosive warhead and were accurate enough to be very effective against a large static target like a fire base.

When the Viet Cong or NVA choose to mount a harassing attack on the large, heavily defended American firebases, like Eagle, the 122 mm rockets were the weapon of choice. They could, and did, cause considerable casualties and destruction of aircraft or facilities. While some 122 rocket attacks were also combined with mortar attacks or even coordinated with assaults, more often they were used alone. I had a very healthy respect for them.

The attack typified much of the Vietnam experience: seemingly endless hours of routine duty under very unpleasant conditions that were then suddenly interrupted by a short intense stretch of unanticipated terror. But after the debris from the attack was cleaned up, the routine reasserted itself and one's thoughts turned to home - to events back in the world - as it always did when you were off duty.

I'm still amazed at how I would mentally shut out the war by focusing on the future beyond Vietnam. My letters always seemed to show that I wanted to look beyond the immediate situation.

Chapter 5 A Tourist of Sorts

Within a few weeks my routine had lapsed back into the dreary, daily grind mixed in with the Army banalities that I found so depressing and so emotionally draining. Here is another part of my letter to the Turners from March 12-15:

> March 15
> ...In between the time I began this letter & now I was in my first rocket attack. (On Friday the 13th - if one is superstitious then the date is important.) By some miracle there was no one injured (other than a few cuts & bruises) even though the buildings received direct hits. The difference between life and death was measured in feet and seconds - a few more (or less) and we would have had many casualties. Altogether 11-12 rockets hit - almost all in group. (And all those hit within a hundred yards of the dispensary - where I happened to be on duty that night.)

We have a very good bunker there, but it didn't seem thick enough then.

Today, a day later, things are back to normal. I have taken Sunday afternoon off to write letters. Afternoons like this I enjoy the area around my bed which I have assembled into what amounts to my "living space". It contains an area (piece of plywood) to write on, a chair, bookshelves (old ammo crates) and a fan....

I have, in my usual pack-rat manner, managed to assemble a collection of assorted goodies which include books, drawing pads, ink, pens, brushes, Japanese acrylic paints, etc. I don't (as I said) get much chance to use them (though I do a great deal of reading) but they are there when I want them. (Which is a comfort.)

For luxuries I have (as mentioned) the fan, a portable radio (which on a good night, I can pick up the Australian relay of the BBC) and the use of the hootch refrigerator (to cool my beer!) And every so often I get together with someone in the hootch & hire a girl to do our laundry.

So except for getting shot at and rocketed every so (very) seldom, duty here is probably better than in the States...

Truely - I feel that I have been sent into exile. More often I feel like I am interred in a (benevolent) forced labor camp rather than at war. (Except for the obvious moments like the other night.)

I really know less of whats going on over here than you do. (As my sources of information are limited. The Stars and Stripes, the Army newspaper is very slanted & gives us only one point of view.) From what I have seen however I am more convinced than ever that what we are doing here is a gigantic mistake. We have despoiled the land and the people. We seem to export the very worst of our culture.

My best,

Andy

The war went on and on with no seeming meaning or progress - it was happening and I was part of it but there didn't seem to be any good reason for me to be there except that I had my orders. My DEROS date seemed so far away and it was all very depressing. While I certainly didn't want to see any hostile action, I was hungry for anything out of the ordinary routine. Anything out of the ordinary was interesting and a unique kind of tourist experience for me was worth writing about:

Betsy & Steve

Thanks for the letter. I'm glad to hear you're busy - I suppose the problems are part of the norm. (At least you're busy enough to have them!)

Went on a tour of Hue last Sunday: to the old Citadel & inner city & then to a couple of temples. Probably the only tour I'll ever go on where everyone carried a M-16 & full ammo load along with their cameras! At any rate it was interesting - not spectacular. Found a crafts shop (government sponsored) on the tour & will get back shortly to buy some pottery & perhaps a small (antique) relief I spotted. Hopefully I'll find some more items of interest. At any rate the pottery is somewhat interesting - commercial & export oriented.

I guess I'm close to hitting rock bottom emotionally about now. Not that I'm morbidly depressed - but it just seems so damned long before I get out of this god damned war & army.

Its starting to get warm here, the monsoon is almost over. The temperature was up to 99 degrees in my area. According to the "old timers" its going to get a lot hotter. (But they say that it cools off at night here to a reasonably comfortable level. (Tonight for instance its down to 80.) I'm afraid by the time I get out of here I shall be hard pressed to adjust to cold. (But I'll be damned glad to see snow!)

Two views of the interior of the Citidal in Hue

132

Which must be almost gone by now.

Andy

That unique tour of Hue was, I think, offered by the local municipal government. As I recall, it was organized in the dispensary. We gathered together a small group of interested soldiers who each paid a small fee and, as a group we were provided a tour guide. We went on this tour in full battle dress, (including small arms and flack jackets but minus helmets). It took us to many parts of the city's historic sites including (as mentioned) the Citadel as well as a number of temples and historic buildings for which Hue was famous.

The temples and historic sites were in varied conditions, some undamaged, some still undergoing major repairs including the still badly damaged Citadel, and the Hue Cathedral . We walked with rifles slung but cameras clicking away. At the end of the tour we ended up being directed to a government-sponsored gift store that was promoting and selling Vietnamese handicrafts. Perhaps the Vietnamese were slow to embrace American style democracy, but American style capitalism had definitely taken hold in Vietnam! I looked at a number of items, but did not buy anything; however, a week or so later, I returned and bought two contemporary ceramic pots, a small Indian bronze relief and a small bronze Vietnamese dragon that was labeled as 19th Century. Both the bronze relief and the dragon were labeled as old (18th & 19th centuries respectively), but on closer examination (after I bought them) that attribution seemed somewhat doubtful as both appeared to have been made much more recently. (Perhaps they had even been cast a only few months before I purchased them and then worked on to give them an "antique" look.) But I liked them anyway and I still have them both.

The ceramic pots also intrigued me and since my father was a potter, as was a long time family friend, Robert Turner, they were impossible to pass up even though they looked like they were produced in a mold (slip cast) and then hand decorated. In letters to my parents and the Turners I describe the pots I am sending them and speculate on the origins. My April 17, 1970 letter to my parents reads, in part:

> *"...Also will be sending you (and the Turners) a package. Vietnamese pottery! Don't know how soon I will send it as that depends on how soon I can get suitable packing material.*
>
> *I got the pottery in Hue at a Government crafts outlet. Its products are for the export trade. The pottery is Western influenced - produced somewhere*

The government crafts shop in Hue.

near Saigon. Couldn't get much out of the salesgirls as they had no English & I had no Vietnamese. (But when I was there a few weeks ago on the tour, I asked the guide.)....

Also bought a couple of small bronzes. One is an Indian 18th Century relief - two figures....the other a small ornamental dragon - Vietnamese 19th Century. Very derivative from traditional Chinese form but again interesting enough to buy...."

It was the first time I had been in Hue for an extended time and so it was fascinating to me, even if the city was still very much in ruins. Since I had grown up and spent most of my life in northern climates, even such mundane things such as the ubiquitous open storefronts were of great interest to me.

Our predecessors in the 101st Airborne who participated in the bitter fighting that created the destruction two years previously would have found this tour grimly ironic.

American and ARVN fought hard in and around the city, and proceeded, with great human sacrifice, to regain every inch of Hue after the NVA and VC occupied it for 25 days during and after Tet of 1968.

Lt. Robert Santos, then a rifle platoon leader with the 101st Airborne, as recorded by Al Santoli in *Everything We Had*, remembered it as a very bitter, almost surrealistic, battle. Lt. Santos was acutely

Another view of the Citidal

aware that it was a civil war and he made reference to his going into the Detroit riots with the 101st before going to Vietnam. But of course, since it was army against army in Hue, the carnage was much higher. (Santoli's book containing Santos account was comprised of oral histories by American soldiers of the Vietnam War.)

Another view of it came from John Laurence, a correspondent and television reporter for CBS news who covered the seige with the Marines of the First Marine Regiment. His memories of it were those of the professional reporter and his narrative of his time there appears in Part One of *The Cat From Hue*, (Public Affairs, 2002). Laurence went in to Hue on February 3 with the Marine reinforcements who were among the first to reach the few Americans still holding on in the two pockets, one around the Citadel, the other at MACV headquarters, where they and the South Vietnamese had desperately and bravely held on. At the ancient Citadel, which was also the South Vietnamese Army headquarters for I Corps, the North Vietnamese had not only penetrated it, but managed to occupy a large portion of it before finally being driven out three weeks later.

Hue, as the ancient capital of Vietnam, was more than just another city. It was a potent symbol and when the North Vietnamese had taken it at the begining of the Tet Holiday in February 1968, they hoped it would be a rallying point for popular support. Even when that failed to materialize, the North Vietnamese held on to it tenaciously for about a month and the fight to recapture it was bitter, involving hand to hand, block by block, house by house fighting with huge casualities and property distruction in the extreme. Laurence graphically describes the carnage and destruction. (He also recounts his own act of redemption in finding and adopting a kitten.)

Two years later, as my photographs indicate, there was still ample evidence of the destruction. What we didn't see however, was evidence of the thousands of casualities - those thousands upon thousands of deaths and injuries visited upon the combatants on both sides as well as upon the civilians and residents of Hue who incurred the savagery of the initial Vietcong and NVA assault and then the counter assault of the combined U.S. and South Vietnamese forces. So, while the NVA units were gone, pushed back toward the Au Shau valley and Laos, leaving behind the greatly weakened VietCong to operate in the shadows, the legacy of the occupation remained.

Boredom

By mid April, I was in a real emotional rut and the days stretched out endlessly.

22 April

Betsy & Steve

Not much to say in this note. Am still waiting for a batch of slides to come back that I took on the tour of Hue. (I'm afraid something has happened to them because slides I have taken after that have already returned!)

Got back into Hue to the Craft Shop & bought some things. One pot going home, another to Harriet & a third to the Turners when I can find some suitable packing. Also got an 18th Century Indian relief & 19th Cent Vietnamese dragon. Both small enough (very small) that I'm keeping here to look at. The ceramics are contemporary - made for export (obviously) & much influenced by Western pottery. But they are hand thrown (although produced on a production line basis I'm sure!) No goodies for you people (but I'm looking) yet!

I try to keep something of interest going, i.e. a project of some sort outside my job. Otherwise I would go mad (and I'm bored & in a bad humor often now). There is nothing here (in the Army) that even vaguely interests me. I look forward to letters, my books & a can of cold beer. That and a quiet night - so I don't start in the middle of it because of artillery, etc.

Will take an R & R in August to Japan (that's about as far in advance as I dare think about.)

23 April

To a certain extent living here acquires an existence independent of anything that exists "back in the

A shop in Hue.

world"! That expression "back in the world" is precisely how one sees things. The "Alice in Wonderland" feeling is now reversed - this is up "out there" is the trip down the rabbit hole. Some people actually have their entire life structured around the existence here. One fellow (who bunked right next to me) had been here for two years - and he was terrified to leave. Scared to go back to the world. It took him a week to get up the courage to leave! Very strange - not really. (But rest assured I shall have no problem leaving here - no indeed!) I can sit here & very vividly think of how much I shall enjoy getting back to NY that winter day!

By the 7th of June I shall be over the halfway mark!

Glad to hear things are not slack. You may not be making any money but things are happening (it sounds like things are!)

Andy

This referred to a kind of normalcy one found in war where the soldier's life took on form, shape and structure that were bizarre and yet so reassuring that some soldiers were reluctant to leave the war. It reflected a kind of weird coping mechanism that human beings have. It seems we all have the capacity to make the bizarre become the mundane - to make the abnormal become normal - and to adjust our reality accordingly. Living in (and with) a war, routine violence (directed at you) can become just a normal part of everyday life. While its timing is unpredictable, the probability and kind of violence is very predictable and thus it can become less threatening than those unknown challenges awaiting you back in the world. The soldier who bunked next to me had become reluctant to leave the structure and value system of Vietnam because he was afraid not of the known - which included danger -but of the unknown and forgotten world of the civilian. He had adjusted so well to the Army system and to his role as a soldier in a war that he had become comfortable with it. He knew what was expected of him whereas back in the world he faced a series of unknown challenges.

Our world was Camp Eagle (or wherever we were) and it was in the US Army in Vietnam - a strange Underworld, complete in and of itself - a Tartarus that existed on the edges of other worlds, including the world of the Vietnamese. Some American soldiers found it hard to leave the Tartarus (the underworld) of the US Army. They had accepted their fate and had adjusted so they could ignore the occasional shelling or rocket attacks. They had found a certain purpose in that strange confined existence with their squad or unit. Part of that security was that most of the time no thinking was required of you as a soldier- you were always given orders. There was a simplicity of existence. Not only was no thinking required of you, but you were cared for by the Army. Its support structures were all essentially self contained. You took care of your buddies and they took care of you - and the omnipotent Army took care of all of us.

American soldiers never really became part of the ongoing daily tradition of life in Vietnam. We never were part of the social structure. We existed parallel to that society or we violently intruded into it. Americans never had relatives on both sides of this war, nor had we watched foreigners come and occupy our country for decades. For the Vietnamese, it was the French coming and occupying the country in the 19th Century, then it was the Japanese (briefly), then the French again (also briefly) and finally the Americans. In all cases the foreigners were there to impose their will. Of all the occupiers, the Americans were

Boys pushing a wagon

probably the least integrated - the most self contained - and consequently the most remote.

There was the strange time/space warp that seemed to afflict many of us in Vietnam. When you got sent to Vietnam, you fell, like Alice, through the looking glass and ended up in a world that didn't resemble the one you had left behind but it was one you had come to terms with. The irrational structure underlying war and your part in that war had become visible to you and you had mastered it. The rational structure of life "back in the world" had disappeared from your view and you couldn't remember it clearly. You knew the real world still existed because you heard news of it and people you had once known there wrote you letters. You knew you would have to face it again someday - if you survived - but you worried about your ability to master it again and to feel comfortable with its complexities. Life in the army was so simple: you did your job, you tried to stay alive and you tried to escape the boredom - when you could. If you couldn't escape the boredom, you gave yourself over to it and you surrendered to it.

While escaping the boredom, or surrendering to it, I was also writing my mother and father about filing my taxes! Yes, we were taxed on your salary as a soldier and although we were not required to file a return while in Vietnam, eventually we had to file. So, ignoring things around me, I wrote about things going on with my other life (back in the world):

> *Enclosed are my tax forms. I do not have to file this year. Just put them somewhere safe - my withholding statement inside also.*
> *Also membership renewal for York State Craftsmen. Please send the $5 - I will be sending you more money toward the car & general expenses.*

I can't write a check - yet. I sent a treasury check to my NY account but I don't know what the situation is! That is to say - the finance office here mails the check. They will not let you. Afraid of currency manipulation. Still have not mailed the pottery. Maybe a week or more before I do!

Hope Grandmother & Mother got to Mobile.

Andy

A few days in May

Two weeks later, and before I could mail the pottery, fate intervened and the war gave me a vivid illustration of how - when one least expects it - shit happens. In a very cryptic letter sent to my parents (without even a salutation), I gave them the news in a carefully worded, and very understated way :

3 May

Shortly you will probably see in the Times that Camp Eagle got hit again last night.

Unfortunately I'm one of the few casualties. Nothing real serious - but I have a banged up knee with a few stitches in it. They are afraid of possible complications so I shall be here a day or so.

Large attack - 8 helicopters, a hanger and our mess hall among other things! That's about it - oh yes. The pottery I have was partially packed & though there was much knocked off shelves the pottery is unharmed...

5 May

Held on to the letter hoping I would have something more to add. But nothing. Still in hospital. Knee looked good yesterday - feels good. Hope I will be out by tomorrow!

Have written to Betsy & Steve but don't have their address here with me - so probably will hold off mailing it (for a day or so).

I laugh now to see how even while I was a casualty, I expressed almost as much concern for the pottery as for anything else, including my own body. The letter also reveals I was strangely relieved, for while I had gotten hurt, in another way I felt my luck held (so it seemed to me) since I wasn't hurt too badly. In the letter to Betsy and Steve, I gave them more details than I had previously given my parents :

5 May

Betsy & Steve

I hope this gets to you - I don't have my address book with me.

Am in the hospital recovering from a knee wound which is not too serious. Eagle was hit by another rocket attack two days ago & unfortunately I'm one of the casualties. Not that a rocket got me but as I was trying to get to a bunker I managed to hit a bit of armour plate with my knee. A bit more than that actually but not very serious really - I have been here 3 days now & should get out tomorrow. Should be off crutches in a week or so.

Meanwhile I'm going out of my mind in this G-D hospital.

By the way, the attack here was costly in terms of materials - 5 Cobras, 3 Chinooks, a hanger, our mess hall & assorted other goodies.

At any rate you know what is happening in case they are upset in Almond. As they probably will be. Will write again in a few days to let you know how things are going.

Andy

And that was the way I put it in the letters. What I remember of those chaotic and terrifying moments, was that I was relieved to be alive but was bleeding from my left leg. It appeared that I had some small cuts on and below the left knee. While the knee hurt, I could still move, albeit painfully, and so I went up to the dispensary. Dave was already there. He had a cut in his upper arm. Two of them were at the dispensary with Dave and others quickly arrived. None of the other medics were injured. We weren't sure it was over; a lull and then a second salvo of rockets were possible. I picked the crud out of my knee, looking for any embedded metal (shrapnel), and carefully cleaned the cuts and put a bandage over them. Once the all clear sounded, the dispensary started filling up with a long line of people who had suffered some misfortune during the attack. Then, in the chaos that followed with the rush of men coming into the dispensary - all with various cuts, broken bones, bruises and other problems that always followed an attack - I worked on others, oblivious to my own problems for the next couple of hours.

About 9 AM, after thing calmed down, I looked at myself again and discovered that I was still bleeding. We couldn't make it stop with any amount of pressure. We didn't have a doctor at that time and we were out of sterile suture sets so Dave sent me off to the Division hospital. At the hospital a doctor took one look at the knee, popped a needle with 100cc of Demerol in my arm and told me to lie still and shut up. He did a bit of surgery, opening the wound up and attempted to tie off a bleeding vein. Unfortunately, when he went in to clamp off the bleeder, they clamped the forceps on a nerve ganglia by mistake - nerve ganglia and small veins look quite similar. Despite 100cc's of Demerol in me, it still hurt like hell and I let them know they had screwed up. They reconnoitred, took the forceps off the nerve ganglia, clamped off the bleeder and tied off the vein. After carefully watching them successfully tie off the vein and sew up the wounds, I went to sleep. I stayed in the hospital only a few days, but I was eager to get out as quickly as possible. I got out before the doctor wanted to release me because my company commander pressed to get me back in the dispensary. We were without a doctor at the time and some of my expertise was both needed and appreciated.

Dave and I agreed that we were both lucky that our problems weren't more serious. He recovered quickly and I walked with crutches for a week or so and then with a cane for a few more. As mentioned, our mess hall took a direct hit and was destroyed and so was my mural. (I hadn't even gotten around to taking a picture of it!)

That night was a typical attack with the 122's coming in late in the night - after 4 AM in two parts. The first salvo was very powerful, and was followed by a lull - then with people thinking that it was all clear, a second wave of rounds came in after people had started to leave the (relative) safety of bunkers.

Not only did we lose Cobra's that night but several of the hits on the Cobras set off their rockets which caused additional havoc! One of the guys in the bed next to me at the hospital had been hurt from one of the exploding rockets from our own Cobra helicopters - not from one of the Viet Cong's 122s!

When the attacks occurred, we were the center of the target for rocket attacks. I don't mean just Camp Eagle (which obviously was the target) but the 101st Aviation Group area appeared to be targeted specifically for these rocket attacks. I'm sure that this was because the helicopters we maintained and flew were so central to the unique strength and capabilities of the 101st Airborne Division. The opportunity to impair or disrupt our ability to fly or coordinate the flying of the Division's helicopters made us a prime target and ensured that we were a target worthy of expending the Viet Cong's limited resources.

Around the dispensary there was something of a bad joke going around for a time that if I was on night duty then our chances of getting hit that night or the next dramatically increased. The jokes about the increased probability of our getting hit (rocketed) on those nights when I happened to be on watch were somewhat based on fact. I was the medic on duty several nights when we got hit - or they hit the night following my duty.

Mortars were also used by the NVA in attacks on the larger US bases, frequently in conjunction with the 122 mm rockets, and sometimes suicide squads of sappers also attempted to penetrate the US base perimeter defense system. However, by 1970 in the costal area around Hue controlled by the 101st, these were rare occurrences.

Out in the western mountains and valleys of the Au Shau region, near the Laotian border, where we did not control the area, it was a different story. The North Vietnamese were operating in strength there, and full scale assaults, combining rockets, artillery, mortars and infantry (sometimes even using armor) on US firebases were still common.

Chapter 6 The Long Summer

June 1970

11 June

Betsy & Steve

    Your trip to Harrisburg sounded good. The pool table exquisite.
    Happy Birthday, Betsy - with a little luck you'll get a (considerably) late B-d present.
    Not much to say from here. I (of course) have been rather restricted in my activity & haven't been outside Camp in a month and a half. My knee is not progressing - (it looks like I'm stuck with a scar.) will probably have to use the cane for another month or so. Not that I have problems walking - I don't. But I can't kneel & haven't dared try running. I shall go out to the beach [Eagle Beach our in-country R & R center] this

weekend & if the water cooperates shall see if I can swim (sedately). I suppose I shall just wait & see. (Haven't talked to the Dr. about it recently - I shall shortly.) The other thing about the knee is that it stiffens up after standing on it for an hour or so.

The days have become a long continuous blur - hot and sweaty. Filled with Army stupidity & mindless tasks to be done (eventually). I save my sanity; not by thinking of what is going on back in the world & what I'm missing; but what is going on out in the boonies beyond the wire & I'm thankful that I'm not one of those dusty sweat-stinking paddy-hopping mothers. Here at least I sweat in the shade & don't go looking for contact. Here it comes at night perhaps once a month - there it comes day & night every day.

(I hope you have written Sen. Goodell telling him to keep up the good work.)

Of work - what is Sean going to do for the summer?

Susanjean H. sent me a baby announcement - another daughter. Fantastic - she & Gary sound so happy and very settled. So foreign to what is happening here. Hell, I can't even sleep (deeply) at night for fear the 122's will come in.

Really I am not paranoid - quite pissed off at time though. I think sometimes out of sheer frustration & boredom. Those two commodities comprising the principle [sic] part of my existence here.

Saw an issue of the Village Voice a few weeks ago. A report in it on an artists meeting at which time they discussed how they could effectively protest the war & finally decided to close down (for one day or more) their shows. What a lot of bullshit - who in hell are they going to influence that way.

But of course none of them will go out and produce some practical propaganda like nice juicy anti-war posters.

Ah well - we all have our little problems don't we?!

Andy

Clearly I was frustrated and angry with what I viewed as smugly self-centered people, at being in Vietnam, with my knee for not healing faster and with my situation in general. I was not very tolerant of events like the one reported in the Village Voice: that some artists were demonstrating excessive self-importance, egocentric and self-righteous posturing in opposition to the war. Closing their galleries for one day was certainly not an event even vaguely approaching the magnitude of, for example, Norman Morrison's self-immolation. (To protest the Vietnam War, Mr. Morrison set himself on fire outside the Pentagon on November 2, 1965, and even that shocking event had little or no effect on the war.) To someone sitting in the dusty heat of Vietnam, closing their own exhibitions for a day seemed an action almost obscenely conceited and self indulgent. My sarcasm, while perhaps a bit petulant, was genuine and deeply felt. After all, I was putting my life on the line. They were putting on airs.

I was angry and my knee was stiff and uncooperative. I was using a cane but was pretty much back to normal in my routines but with some limited mobility. At least, I was feeling well enough to be ornery and to bitch about the boring routine. I had been there more than six months now and I could begin to think about the light at the end of my personal tunnel.

In contrast to the artists self indulgent gestures, I did support the efforts of someone like Senator Charles Goodell, a U.S. Senator from New York, who dedicated much of his Senatorial career to opposing the Vietnam War and who ended up sacrificing his political career by doing so. Events back in the world were very, very important to all of us in Vietnam. While we didn't hear about many events, we did get some news and we paid attention to what we heard, since by 1970 it was pretty clear that many - if not most - Americans did not want the war to continue. Richard Nixon, after all, had been elected in 1968 on a promise to extricate the US. He had begun the Paris Peace talks in January of 1969 and, in June of 1969 announced the policy of "Vietnamization." In May of 1970 widespread protests against the war occurred on US college campuses - including the infamous fatal shootings of students by the Army National Guard at Kent State. In Vietnam, there was a mixture of feelings among American troops that ranged from deep cynicism to extreme patriotism - and on some days, those feelings could exist almost simultaneously in each of us. We were not mercenaries - we were citizen soldiers. We wondered why we were the ones fighting a war that certainly didn't have strong public support, but we were also proud of the job that each of us was doing - and we all wanted to be doing something that was in our country's best interest.

A few days after I wrote the above letter, our new flight surgeon arrived and he advised me to just start walking; "throw away the cane," he said, "put weight on the knee, and exercise it back to normal." I did so immediately.

> *June 17*
> *Hi*
> *Just in case you're interested your airmail letter took five days to get here & the last 1st Class took seven days so I guess the Airmail really is faster.*

Delighted to see the bit on the "hay knife". [An antique tool.]

Glad to hear Grandmother enjoyed my note. Will try to send her another shortly - let me know if her address changes. I'm very sorry to hear that they don't feel she will improve. [She had fallen and broken her hip in Mobile and had begun to go down hill immediately.]

I sent off the Vietnamese pot to you yesterday so sometime in the next month it should arrive. I hope it arrives safely.

You ask "which knee"? The left one - and I am walking around unaided now. A bit stiff but not bad. A pretty good scar I'm afraid though.

Very hot, very long, and very boring are the days. June & July look like they are going to be very long months. In August I am going to Japan on an R & R. After that I'll be able to see the end.
But right now it looks a long, long ways away.
   Andy

Home - my space in the hootch

It seemed that the months could not pass fast enough for me. I was at the middle of my year-long tour of duty but what remained of it seemed to stretch out in front of me forever. Looking forward to the August R & R made it seem manageable. The days and evening were a blur of boredom - with spurts of action. Many of the evenings, when things were quiet, were spent sitting on top of the sandbagged revetments that ringed our hootch, drinking warm beer or soda and talking about our plans for when we got home, about our R & R's (past or anticipated), or about events back in the world while we watched the stars, listened to (and nervously watched) the action on the berm line and covered our ears every time the 175's roared as they launched another harassing or interdiction round towards the Au Shau in support of a remote fire base or a company dug in a nightly defensive position.

Then we would retreat to our own little private areas to read, write letters home or listen to music and think our own private thoughts before falling into a uneasy, sweaty sleep inside a mosquito net and, if the electricity was working, with a fan trained on us trying in vain to alleviate the oppressive heat.

Training Vietnamese troops in rapelling

Part of the Pacification/Vietnamization effort that we were involved in (after the policy of "Vietnamization" was articulated) was training the Vietnamese to take over a larger part of the fighting - after all it was a war for their country. "Vietnamization" was somewhat late in being implemented. (After all, we had committed the first combat troops to Vietnam in 1965 and had, during the more than four years since then, largely behaved as if it was a US war - not a Vietnamese one. (Since that time, many critics of the Vietnam War have insisted that this was one of the primary errors, along with underestimating the resolve of the enemy, in our Vietnam strategy.) Since that fateful day in 1965, when we first committed large numbers of combat ground troops, we had largely pushed the ARVN troops into a secondary role as Americans took on the responsibility for not only planning and logistics, but also for the conduct of all the major engagements. Belatedly we were now starting to do more in the way of joint training with the announced aim of reversing that strategy. As a result there was much more effort spent on training the Vietnamese to take on a larger burden of the war.

Since my mobility was somewhat limited for duty purposes, I didn't go out on patrol or on Medcaps during this time. But I went along as the company medic with the Pathfinders when they were training the South Vietnamese troops on a couple of occasions. Since the division had somewhat pulled back on its aggressive pursuit of the NVA, the Pathfinders were now spending a portion of their time training the troops of the 1st ARVN Division (based in Hue) in anticipation of them shortly taking over many of the responsibilities and tasks previously shouldered by the Americans.

Among the skills that the Pathfinders were teaching the ARVN troops were those they would need for airborne helicopter assaults. In heavy jungle, even the agile Hueys couldn't always land, so an alternate method of inserting troops was to rappel down a rope from a hovering helicopter. This was one of those innovative techniques that had been developed to take advantage of the unique capabilities of the helicopter-borne infantry, allowing skilled troops to be inserted rapidly without having to prepare a landing zone. This way, troops could still be inserted quickly when the helicopter couldn't land. The chopper would hover a hundred feet or so above the ground while the infantry rappelled down a rope. While it might sound slow, with practice skilled troops could be inserted very quickly since a trained trooper could drop very fast.

The Vietnamese soldiers were mostly young conscripts - not professional soldiers, and they were very unsure of themselves so rappelling was an exercise they found daunting. They were understandably somewhat skittish about doing it. But they got a big kick out of seeing American soldiers demonstrate the rappelling technique, and they were reassured by watching us demonstrate it before they had to attempt it. Not only did they want to watch the Pathfinders show off their well honed skills,

The Division newspaper of February 16, 1970 with my comments written on it.

but they were very eager to see me (the medic) also demonstrate that I could descend along a rope! I think they believed that if someone like me could do it (I was obviously not as skilled as were the Pathfinders) - and survive it - then they too could do this part of the training! While the 101st Airborne incorporated helicopters seamlessly into its operations, the use of this sophisticated tool was not yet a part of the normal everyday activities of the Vietnamese Army! (Nor would it ever be - American piloted and maintained helicopters would be used to support the South Vietnamese army until 1973 when we pulled out almost all the support for the ARVN troops.) I enjoyed the training sessions as they broke the normal routine.

A brief episode

One night in the middle of June, I had been up at the dispensary (but not on duty) and came back to the hootch early in the evening not long after sunset, but before the others had returned. The hootch was quiet, mostly dark and seemingly empty. As I entered and headed for my area which was approximately in the middle of the hootch, I passed next to the spaces nearest the door which were occupied, on the left, by Royce (who was away on a mission) and on the right by Charlie, our baby faced, young Pathfinder medic. When I opened the door and stepped in, someone stepped behind me and something was pressed violently up against the back of my head. It was immediately apparent that it was a gun muzzle. The person, pushing the pistol harder against my head, started screaming curses, ranting at me in an almost incoherent stream of words with a strangely hysterical pitch in his voice. In a flash I realized it was Charlie. I just stood there frozen for a moment (probably it was less time than a minute but it seemed a long time), listening to the stream of words that poured out of him. I finally understood what he was saying: that I was after him, that I was out to get him, and that he was going to blow my motherfucking head off. He was going to blow me "motherfucking away." I said (in my calmest voice), "Hey, wait a minute man..." but he just screamed another obscenity, yelled that I wasn't going to get him and cocked the pistol which he had continued to shove up against the back of my head. Still using my calmest voice, without moving or trying to turn around, I said, "Charlie - whats wrong? Why are you mad at me? What did I do to you? Tell me why you're mad at me?" After a few more obscenities, his voice became quieter and the gun came off the back of my head.   Now, he began to mutter almost incoherently in a low voice. The hysteria was gone as was the anger.

I stepped away, turned around very slowly and carefully, and looked at him. He was still holding the cocked pistol but now, he held it limply and it was pointing at the ground. Again, using my quietest, calmest voice, I said; "Charlie, what's wrong? Why are you mad at me? What did I do to you?" He didn't look directly at me, but looked away over my shoulder; his eyes were glassy and vacant - clearly, he was either on dope or on hard drugs. (Charlie was known to smoke a lot of dope but none of us had never seen him do hard drugs although for the last few days he had seemed "hyper.") He didn't really say anything, but seemed to visibly sag and muttered something that I didn't understand while he continued to point the gun at the floor between his legs. Then he looked down, seemingly ashamed. I said, "Charlie, what did I do to you? Please give me the gun and tell me what's wrong?"

He gave me the gun without resisting - it was my 45, cocked and loaded with one in the chamber and a full clip. Then, he sat down on his cot and put his head in both his hands and sort of whimpered, almost like a child. I jacked the slide back on the

.45, unloaded the round from the chamber, dropped the clip out and put both in my pants pocket along with the gun. Then I sat down next to Charlie and repeated my question; "What's wrong, Charlie?" He didn't answer, he just sort of slumped down, rolled over on his cot in a fetal position and seemed to fall asleep. At that point, one of the other medics came into the hootch - I think it was Jim and I told him about what had happened. Charlie was sound asleep now so we just covered him with his poncho liner and left the hut. We went up to the dispensary in search of whoever else might be there. I was still utterly stunned at this point, but also still (amazingly) calm.

After talking it over with the others, we decided that he must have been high on drugs - probably a combination of something, perhaps amphetamines - and the only place we thought he could have gotten amphetamines was from the escape and evasion kits that were stored in the pharmacy at the dispensary. So we looked, and sure enough, when we checked the escape and evasion kits, all the amphetamines were gone. It seemed clear Charlie had gotten into them there, and then, feeling paranoid, had picked up the pistol as well. Since I was the (unofficial) pharmacist, that space was one I had the responsibility for and kept organized. It was also where I kept my medical pack stashed and ready to go on patrol or for an emergency. It was packed not only with supplies but also with the .45 that Jaster had given me. That was probably why he thought I was after him since I believe he felt I was on to him - whether for stealing the pistol or taking the amphetamines (or both) wasn't clear - nor at that point did it really matter. In his delusionary, paranoid state, he was feeling threatened and trapped - and the pistol was the weapon at hand so he took it. And then, when I walked in on him in the hootch, the amphetamine-fueled paranoia took over.

The next morning Charlie was very apologetic and told me over and over how sorry he was. And, not too surprisingly, things went back to the way they had been. Charlie behaved well, was cooperative and helpful and no one mentioned the incident again. He continued going out with the Pathfinders as much as he could (almost daily) until the day a few weeks later when a Pathfinder was shot through the head and killed right next to him as they returned fire in a brief firefight. That event shook Charlie's belief in his own invulnerability and he was deeply affected by it. Subsequently he became more subdued, and much more cautious. After that, while he went out on some Pathfinder missions, he was also much more willing, even eager on occasion, to spend more time in the dispensary. But wherever he was, we now kept careful tabs on our medicines - particularly ones that could be abused. Fortunately, there were no more bad incidents involving Charlie and drugs.

Half Way

In early July, as I passed my midway date, I wrote home to reassure everyone that my knee wasn't as bad as my disposition. My mood was not upbeat, not so much because of the knee, but mostly because it was very, very hot in Vietnam and I felt I had been there forever trapped in limbo. I remember how the days, which stretched endlessly in front of me, seemed to be hot, sweaty and dusty, and to hold ever more of the same boring routines. However, just about the time things had settled into a hot, dull and boring routine, we got jolted out of our complacency by the Viet Cong. During the monsoon season, the ability of both sides to move men and supplies and conduct operations was somewhat limited. For the Americans, heavily dependent on helicopters and motorized vehicles, the heavy rains definitely limited offensive operations, but they did so for the NVA as well. But, after the monsoon season was over, the land had dried out and that meant that hostile activity increased on both sides.

July 2

Hi,

Thanks for the pictures - it is hard to imagine a change of seasons. The weather has been very much the same since March - gradually getting hotter but otherwise the same.

When I wrote Betsy I was in a bad mood - I didn't mean to make my knee sound too terrible. I mean, it has healed as much as it shall. I do have a considerable scar and it get stiff at times. I'm not using cane, etc. any more. It sure as hell isn't as good as new but it won't make me a cripple for life either. I did get a letter from Karen Cushing and answered it - she must have been delighted - I got another one. Laurie

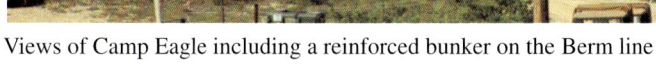

Views of Camp Eagle including a reinforced bunker on the Berm line

Murray & Kathy Young did write - what they call their "end of the year report"! (No - they had not written before.) [These girls were all former students of mine.]

By the way your two letters arrived the same time. (Pkg #37 has arrived also.)

Not too much to report - we got hit with mortars and 7 rockets last week. Both the same night; about midnight & then just about when everyone was settling down the rockets came in. The mortars landed on the other side of camp & I even got a chance to put on some clothes before going to the bunker. But the rockets were right down the alley & I didn't waste time with clothes after the first one landed. There were some casualties but none in group.

Otherwise things have been quiet.

Andy

In reading my letters from this time, it's clear that hostile actions had become routine - I don't even make rocket attacks the first item of news home or even make it a major concern in the next letter. In hindsight, I am struck by the fact that I mentioned the rocket attacks in such a matter-of-fact way, almost in passing, with the sense of the event being little more than an annoyance. I was more pleased to report on some letters I'd gotten from some of my former students, and a couple from home.

I guess I had a lot of explaining to do about the pessimistic letter of June 11 to Betsy & Steve. So, after writing to my parents I also wrote Betsy and Steve a day later, explaining my state of mind when I wrote that previous letter to them.

6 July

Hi,

Apparently I was in a very bad mood when I wrote the last time. My damned knee is healed & it works albeit stiffly at times. I stopped using a cane a few days after I wrote you last. It has healed but I have a scar & as I said its stiff at times & aches. But it works.

We got hit again last week & it got me to the bunker. Bad night - we got hit twice in the same night. About midnight with mortars & then about 3 AM just as everyone was getting back to sleep we got hit with 122s (rockets). The mortars came in on the other side of camp & I got dressed before going to the bunker. But the rockets were right down the alley again & sent us to the bunker pronto without clothes.

Bad night. The mortar attack caused casualties inc. a couple of fatalities. The rockets got a couple of ship(s). There was also a minor ground probe.

It was not serious in Group - no serious injuries.

I'm not trying to scare you - it doesn't happen that often. (But I do feel I earn my hazardous duty pay.)

Most of the time though is utter boredom. Long hot days.

7 July

More rockets - only 4 last night but that was enough to wake me up & send me to the bunker. Was on CQ again & one hit close enough to the dispensary to shower the roof with shrapnel & cut the power line from our generator. This morning I picked up lots of shrapnel around the dispensary. Getting to be a bit much - twice in less than 10 days. Its also the second *time we've gotten hit when I've been on CQ - the other two times were the night after I had it.*

That's a bit much also.

Sec. of State [William] Rogers in Saigon now, says 97% of Vietnam is secure! (Un-huh! Say it again - Bill!)

One good thing - we saw "Butch Cassidy & the Sundance Kid" two nights ago! It was one of those rare films worth seeing over here. (A film is shown every night - I've gone 7 times in the 7 months I've been here!)

No power down here because of the rocket & the thermometer in my area says 104 & the one at the other end of the hootch 110. My day off & no cold beer nor even a fan! That R & R to Japan next month is looking better & better.

Sean must have done quite a bit of work while he was there. At least it must have been good for him.

I got a few snapshots from Mother last week of Almond - it looks wonderful. Also a letter from Uncle Bill telling about a fishing trip to Porcupine. Reminded me - this was the first Spring in over 20 years I didn't do any fishing!

Andy

My cryptic, and sarcastic, comments about the Secretary of State reflected the cynicism that most American soldiers reserved for the official government statements on the war. But it also reflected the shameless degree of public dishonesty or denial that existed then in Washington. Most soldiers in Vietnam believed that the American government did not speak truthfully about any aspect of the war at that time. Why the

Government wasn't more openly honest remains a mystery to me today. Because of what they viewed as cynical governmental dishonesty, American soldiers grew to utterly distrust their own Government's public statements - and its conduct. As a result of that, thirty years later, there are probably a huge number of ex-GI's who continue to have the same feelings of distrust and cynicism about the government and its public pronouncements.

Spec 5 Thomas Pellaton, then working in the 101st Avn Group intelligence section, certainly knew more than I did about the overall situation in the 101st's area of operations. He wrote a letter at that time, dated 28 July 1970, that, in part, described the situation out at Fire Support Base Ripcord (near the Au Shau) and provided some insights into the mood of many G.I.'s at the time.

He wrote passionately of the human costs of our strategy of contesting the NVA for territory out in the wilds of Vietnam's border area with Laos where the Ho Chi Min Trail was located. He was particularly bitter about the failure of Vietnamization and about the lack of enthusiasm displayed by the South Vietnamese soldiers who seemed to care little about their own cause. To him, the costs in American lives (the letter mentions more than 80 killed and 420 wounded in a two week period) caused by an American failure of leadership that kept the troops in a one night defensive position for five or six nights allowing the NVA to mass forces around them, was a very tragic result of our inability to develop the strategy (and execute it) of Vietnamization.   *(The letter is quoted in Dear America, pg. 228)*

Indeed, ensuring that the responsibility for the war moved from America to the South Vietnamese proved elusive. But, Pellaton eloquently asked the same question in that letter that many GI's were privately asking each other daily. Namely, we asked what were we doing there in a war that was increasingly recognized as marginally important to our country and yet, was deeply devisive. (These events followed closely on the heels of the Kent State tragedy of May 1970 when National Guardsmen killed several protesting college students.)

Eagle Beach -the In country R & R Center

In my June 11 letter I mentioned Eagle Beach. Eagle Beach was the in-country R & R Center for the 101st, located on a strip of lovely beach on Vin Loc Island, that long costal island south of Hue where we also ran a lot of medcaps in the more remote areas. Eagle Beach, run by the division, was a strange place which tried to combine an Army base with a resort! It had a lovely sandy beach facing the South China Sea, where you could swim in lovely warm Gulf of Tonkin water while guards in towers on the highly fortified berm line behind you watched (you hoped) the countryside inland for any signs of hostile forces. (Normally, it was pretty quiet on that part of the island.) Besides swimming, there were speed boats for water skiing.

A Cobra flies over the entrance to the TOC

The "resort" also had a small PX, a mini-golf course, pool tables, stages for USO entertainers, massage parlors and seahuts made into very rudimentary bars and entertainment facilities, complete with local Vietnamese bargirls serving and entertaining the soldiers. Unfortunately, as a medic, I treated a number of soldiers that had contacted particularly nasty cases of venereal disease during their stays at Eagle Beach.

Complete with barracks and a mess hall, troops could spend a few days there on a rotational basis. It was largely used by the division to provide some "down time" for those troops that had been stationed for a long time on remote firebases or out on active "search and destroy" operations and needed time to relax.

Those troops usually got flown in by helicopter, but you could also drive down to it from Eagle, crossing from the mainland via a rickety ferryboat. It was a lovely drive there from Eagle,

Dave on the beach at Eagle Beach

Back to New Orleans

We left Eugene's tale shortly after the surrender of Port Hudson. He wrote in his diary on July 15:
Have received cheering intelligence from the North if true. All quiet today, cool and cloudy.
(Vintage, pg 198)

This was almost certainly a reference to Gettysburg which had happened about the same time as the Seige of Port Hudson was entering its final days. Two weeks later, near New Orleans he writes:
Monday, August 3. I was occupied this forenoon cleaning my gun and this afternoon I went down to the city with Lt. Kimball. I found my knapsack which I had left at New Town, but it had been robbed of its contents....
(Vintage, pg. 201)

He was back in familiar surroundings. The next day he wrote his brother:
Dear Brother,

Once more we are in the vicinity of New Orleans. It has been eight months since we left for active service and we have had some pretty hard times in the course of events. We have marched about 500 miles, fought as the road followed the Perfume river much of the way and passed a number of previously elegant, and now rundown, French style villas from the 19th Century and the era of colonial occupation. There were also a few strikingly handsome, although now somewhat rundown, Buddhist Temples on the river.

I also remember one trip to Eagle Beach when we were at the end of a convoy of trucks when a very small Vietnamese toddler wandered out into the road and was struck by one of the trucks. We came to a screeching halt and jumped out into a swarm of wailing and angry Vietnamese civilians milling around the supine and seemingly comatose child. Fighting our way through, and fending off a syringe wielding relative, we got a chance to examine the child and discovered that by some miracle, he (or she, I've forgotten) had not been run over; but he had walked into the tire of the speeding truck and had been knocked backwards (and made briefly unconscious) but, except for several bruises, was unhurt!

Temple on the Perfume River.

Entertainers and Entertainment

The 101st Aviation Group had a stage built into a hillside forming a kind of natural amphitheater where the visiting USO entertainers performed and where the weekly "special" movies were shown. The ordinary movies (very, very bad) were shown every night in the mess hall - when there was power - and barring any hostile activity that might preclude it. The USO entertainers and special visitors came less frequently - perhaps once a month or every three to five weeks. (It was not on a regular basis.) Those visitors were a strange mixture of country and western or rock bands, sometimes combined with vaudeville acts or other miscellaneous performers. The movies were generally deadly dull and seemed to have been selected most often to serve as a diversion or for propaganda purposes. Sometimes that would backfire - I remember the reaction of the troops to the showing of the movie The Green Berets (starring John Wayne) which was shown soon after I arrived. The soldiers started hooting John Wayne when he appeared and then later cheered during the scenes when the Green Berets were being attacked and even during the scene when they take casualties. They just couldn't take the Hollywood version of our war seriously - from their vantage point it was a crock of crap. There was also a standard admonition from officers or sergeants before going out on patrols "Now listen up you guys, I don't want any fucking John Waynes out there....you just do what you are supposed to do."

The live USO entertainment and performance nights were also seldom very interesting, and while many times I completely ignored them, sometimes out of sheer boredom I would go and watch for a while. One memorable night I watched a Philippine Rock Band playing American rock music (not very well, as I recall). That night I was sitting high up on the hill of

three battles and been all through the seige of Port Hudson. It has been seven months since we were paid.... Our Company when we went up to Port Hudson numbered 30 effective men, and we lost 18 killed and wounded, over half as you see. We saw some pretty hard rubs....
(Vintage, pgs. 201 and 202)

His company had suffered pretty heavy loses at Port Hudson, but they were not given any time to reflect on that but were shipped out to a new front immediately after Port Hudson surrendered. One of the things that astounded me about Eugene's experience was the mobility his unit had. True, he had marched more than 500 miles, but it was also true that he had traveled many more miles by train or on ships. Units were moved from area to area and from theatre to theatre, as he would shortly find out! Quite a contrast to our "airmobile" yet immobile division!

"That is the way,..."

As a digression, it was interesting to read about the great abundance of food that was available in the New Orleans area, either by purchase or

169

frequently by "foraging". Eugene's company, like many, roamed the countryside and so he was often able to procure supplemental rations. In a letter to his father, Eugene writes:

..We had a tip top time coming down we have a good camping ground in the center of the village and the way we confiscate chickens, geese, turkeys, sugar, etc., etc., is a caution. That is the way, first we live on hard bread and water and then on the fat of the land and then we have to go back to bread and water again.... (Vintage pg. 134)

And, in the letter to his mother, he describes fare, not ordinarily available in Maine:

...We have plenty of fish and shrimp here, and oranges in any quantities. We can go out into the country a little way and get as many oranges as we can carry for nothing. We generally manage to eat between 20 and 40 oranges apiece every day.... (Vintage pg 121)

He also writes about going to theatre and musical performances in New Orleans and in one letter describes a performance (that he enjoyed) by John Wilkes Booth.

the amphitheater looking out toward the berm line which was behind the performers on the stage when an alert was sounded and some shooting started on the perimeter and fu gas (very potent tear gas) was also detonated. These were normal nightly events on Eagle, and, unless some heavy duty hostile fire, such as rockets or mortars, started coming back in, no one paid much attention to it. (I always wondered if the visitors ever got used to these things.) So the show went on with only a momentary pause. But there was a light wind blowing in towards us, and since the fu gas was heavier than air it slowly, but steadily moved as a mass along the ground right onto the arena stage where the performers were in the midst of their act. That act ended in pandemonium with much laughter from many of the watching GI's (including me) who had seen it coming but didn't pass on the warning to the performers.

Books

One of the great pleasures for many soldiers in Vietnam was reading. For many soldiers, reading had to do with the need to escape. In the absence of television, books were the answer. I read voraciously as my letters made clear. So did many other soldiers. In fact, books, once read, were placed on a table in the dispensary waiting room where they were taken and replaced by others from those readers' collections. (There was a huge turnover every week!)

Another great pleasure of the soldiers was, of course, music. Every soldier seemed to have his own "boombox" or, at least, a portable radio with a cassette player. The choice of music was individual and varied quite dramatically! (But it was also interesting to hear the variety.)

In relation to that, I should note that there was a group of soldiers among the intelligence EM's, who were opera fanatics. (These included the previously mentioned Tom Pellaton, whose letters appear in *Dear America , Letters Home from Vietnam*. One of those letters recounts his singing an operatic aria while out in a village guarding a MedCap.) They not only not only spent hours listening to opera, but also talked passionately and extensively about it. One night, talking with them over a few warm beers in the EM club, but blithely unaware of their devotion, I made some casual, but obviously intemperate remarks denigrating the importance of opera as an art form and got in serious trouble with them. Subsequently, I was invited back several times to engage in heated, not always friendly debates and arguments about the importance of opera as an art form. It was one of the few times I engaged in a lively and welcome bit of intellectual discussion during the time I spent in the Army - and it was one of the few instances when I didn't feel I had to be careful about revealing my own background and education.

Food

Because it is sometimes one of the few pleasures that may be had during a campaign, soldiers seem to always be concerned about the food that they are fed - or able to forage. If not supplied with good rations, it has been a time-honored practice for soldiers to forage and secure food locally. I was fascinated to read Eugene Kingman's letters as he wrote incessantly about his need to supplement his Army rations by either foraging or buying food from the sutlers who followed the troops from camp to camp during the Civil War.

For the American soldiers in Vietnam - at least for those of us in situations like I was in, food was certainly plentiful and it was

Eugene's final months

After spending the rest of 1863 in the New Orleans area, it probably seemed to Eugene that the worst of the war might be over for the 12th Maine. He wrote home on Christmas, 1863:

I wish you and all the rest a Merry Christmas and I hope you all are having a good time tonight. I wish that I had something to come Santa Claus with, but the most that I can send will be a letter and my good wishes. This is probably the last Christmas that I shall spend in the Army and I am glad of it...
(Vintage, pg. 236)

In January of 1864 Mell Gould, Eugene's best friend, reenlisted - but Eugene did not. (I found it very telling that Eugene choose not to re-enlist.) The first six months of 1864 went peacefully except that Eugene's diary records recurring bouts with swamp fever.

Algiers, New Orleans,
July 8, 1864
Dear Father,
When I last wrote you I was at Morganzia Bend just below red River, but now we are at Algiers opposite New Orleans. We started from Morganzia the third and arrived here the evening

"All American" rather than the rice based, highly spiced Vietnamese diet. The American army tried very hard to be self-sufficient, and so most of the army food was shipped in, not purchased locally. The US armed forces set up a huge logistics operations, with giant resupply bases at Da Nang and Cam Ranh Bay, where ships and cargo planes disgorged huge amounts of supplies - including food and beverages. While the army food in Vietnam was plentiful for most troops in secured locations such as Eagle, it was still pretty boring since much of it was frozen or came in cans. It was much worse for those troops at the end of the supply lines - at remote fire bases or out in the boonies. They lived mostly on canned C-Rations! But even out on relatively isolated firebases, hot food was supplied occasionally - when possible - by helicopters. Food wasn't an issue for me and so I never wrote home about it. Not that it was bad. It wasn't. It was just very predictable and rather boring. Sometimes the food was also obsessively abundant in some ways and the overwhelming availability of certain items - such as roast beef - was irrational and irritating. I vividly remember getting sick of roast beef. Roast beef was supplied so much that the cooks tried every way they knew to prepare it and then invented some new ways, but none-the-less the repetition proved deadly and they couldn't get soldiers to enthusiastically eat it in any form. Potatoes, served in a multitude of ways, were standard fare and so was Jello, which can only be served in a limited number of ways. Bread, waffles and pancakes, as well as cakes and cookies were prepared, but never seemed very interesting. Fresh fruit was supplied - although it was limited in its variety. Apples were relatively common, as were oranges, and there were some locally supplied bananas (very small, but quite sweet) and on occasion some melons. Packages from home with cookies, cakes and other items not easily (if ever) obtainable were treasured.

Holidays

It is interesting to note that while I mentioned Christmas in one letter shortly after I arrived, I don't mention the July 4th holiday. It, and other lesser holidays passed without much notice, although the 4th of July was celebrated by the Army. Of course, the way holidays were celebrated by the troops while in Vietnam was quite different from the way we celebrated them "back in the world." The war didn't stop, so while we got special meals and perhaps the work routine for the day was slightly relaxed, there was no way to escape or forget where you were, and the VC or NVA certainly didn't observe those holidays. In fact, we were on heightened alert during the 4th of July in anticipation of NVA attacks that actually came a few days later. But I do remember seeing a spectacular "fireworks display" the evening of the 4th that was actually a couple of Cobra gunships attacking a suspected enemy position with their mounted mini-guns and automatic 40mm grenades launchers.

In a letter to Mother and Dad a week later, I express my eagerness for news from home about my brother, as well as responding to the need to do something as ordinary as complete a registration form for my car.

> 13 July
>
> Enclosed the completed registration form for the car.
> Glad the pot arrived - the Turners' haven't gotten theirs yet because I just mailed it today. A problem getting boxes to pack with.
> We got hit three times within the past couple of weeks, twice one night & then again last week. Also lots of action both north & west of here.
> Pkg #41 also arrived today. Along with bks.

of the fourth on board a transport in ... .I was taken sick the day before we left and have been in hospital ever since with swamp fever. I am much better now and expect to return to my company tomorrow. They are concentrating a great many men here, the 13th and 14th Army Corps and everything promises a strike somewhere and pretty quick. Some have already left on ocean transports for places unknown and I suppose that we shall leave before long. I received a letter from Mother a few days ago but was too sick to answer it. As for my "love for humanity" I am afraid I do not sympathize as readily now with the suffering of others, ...Three years out here will give a man a great many new ideas and subjects for thought and it is impossible for a man to have as soft a heart after serving in the army three years as before, not that I am hard hearted I trust. I am willing to do every man justice and yet I have compassion on the sufferings of others. In four months I hope to be at home when we can talk these things over.... (Vintage, pg. 286)

He was bitter, and, the end of his enlistment was on his mind and on the 12th of July he wrote in his diary "In three months it will be three years

173

since I enlisted." (Vintage, pg 288.) He was, in the vernacular of the American soldier in Vietnam, a "short-timer"!

By the Summer of 1864, the Civil War was beginning its final phase. Grant, now firmly in charge, was aggressively pursuing his bloody, but effective, strategy of attrition. He was beginning his pursuit of Robert E. Lee's forces and also simultaneously attacking all along the Confederate lines in Northern Virginia, just south and west of Washington.

On July 13 Eugene's regiment was put on board a transport headed for Virginia. Although he was confined to bed in the hospital, Eugene was with them. On the 15th, while still on board the ship, he was discharged from the hospital and rejoined his company. They docked at Fortress Monroe on the 20th and proceeded up river to Bermuda Hundred the next day. Eugene's diary for the 22nd reads:

"We got ordered to march last night at 9 o'clock and we started for the front. We marched about all night and now

Whats Sean doing with himself these days?

Andy

I must have become completely blase about rocket attacks by then. But there is an interesting note on the bottom:

Haven't been able to get more legal size envelopes! If you can find some legal size envelopes that seal by pressure would you send them on. Ordinary legal size envelopes that seal with moisture are no good over here because of humidity!

This request for envelopes that seal by pressure highlights some of the mundane tasks that became difficult because of the extreme humidity in the climate in Vietnam. Ordinary envelopes were useless since they would absorb the moisture from the air and seal themselves shut in no time. And, if the reference to the number 41 package may seem strange, the answer is simple. My father numbered the packages he sent me since it was a simple way to track them. If something didn't arrive I could let my parents know. Having to write home for envelopes was an indication of some of the daily tribulations some GI's faced with ordinary things - both necessities and luxuries. Sometime the luxuries could be very small things indeed.

Sending letters was simple, but sending packages home was considerably more of a chore. Just getting to the base post office, located on the far side of the base, often presented problems. So packages mailed home were a rare occurrence and I think I only did it a couple of times. Here is a reference to one such occurrence:

21 July

Sue & Bob,

Sometime in the next few weeks - if all goes well you should receive a package containing a (commercial) sample of Vietnamese pottery.

I got it way back in April but for one reason or another I never got a chance to ship it until last week. It's a commercial pot produced at a pottery near Saigon. From the looks & price of the pot it was produced specifically for the export/tourist trade. Kind of an interesting combination of bastard Western contemporary design with Eastern sensibility! (At least I found it interesting enough to buy!)

It was purchased in a Government sponsored craft shop which had pottery & lacquer-ware, etc (contemporary) plus antique bronzes. The antique bronzes, while small were quite interesting & I got a couple of them along with the pottery.

My excursions outside Camp Eagle have been very few the last 3-4 months so I don't really have any idea of what the utilitarian ware is like. From what I have seen it is scarce - probably the war having taken its toll (particularly so in the areas I have been in, the outlying parts of Hue which were heavily damaged two years ago.)

Am planning an R & R to Japan next month. Among other things - there I can walk around freely & get a chance to enjoy the countryside! (Am planning to "climb" Mt. Fuji just for the hell of it!)

And when I get back I shall have just about 100 days left here!

find ourselves before Petersburg. I am about used up for I had a very heavy load and I am not very strong." (Vintage, pg. 291)

He wrote his father on the 24th:
"..We have not been here long enough to form much of an opinion as to how things go on. I guess we shall fight a little within four months and I hope we shall take Richmond. It will be a good wind-up for our three years service... " (Vintage, pg. 293)

However, other events proved that prediction, wistful thinking. His diary entries for July 30 and 31:
"Saturday 30. Last night we were routed out at about 12 o'clock and started on the march back to our old camp. We got here about 3 o'clock. It had been an awful warm day and a great many were sun struck on the road."

"Sunday, July 31 Last night about 8 o'clock we were drummed out and marched to Bermuda Hundred and there embarked on board the S.E. Spaulding for Washington. We are crowded very much." (Vintage, pgs. 295-296)

Confederate General Jubal Early was threatening Washington. The 12th Maine was to become part of the hastily constructed defenses for the city.

175

My best to everyone

Andy

The PX

We had a PX on Camp Eagle and every week or so, one of the medics would take a jeep or hitch a ride to it and buy some necessities such as shaving cream, tooth paste (not supplied by the army) and also things considered luxuries such as batteries for our radios, or soda pop and beer, and, for those who smoked, cigarettes. We tried to time the visits so that the selection of beer or soda was still good. In a letter quoted earlier, I mentioned that Budweiser Beer was highly prized and so it, like other choice items, would disappear quickly from the shelves. The Eagle PX was not fancy - it carried the essentials mentioned above, but it did not carry major electronic equipment or cameras or other luxury items unlike some of the other PX's in major areas such as Da Nang or Saigon that assumed almost mythical status for those soldiers who visited them from our division. Those stores were the Army version of that icon of American consumer culture - the department store. For us, the "Big PX" existed only in catalog form - so soldiers spent hours poring over the selections available by mail.

On Eagle, that kind of "in-person" shopping was only a dream and even cold beer or soda was a luxury. Refrigeration was scarce - and while we did have a refrigerator in the dispensary for medicines that needed to be kept cold, we didn't have a refrigerator in the hootch until midway through my tour, so we learned to drink warm beer and soda. Even if it was warm, beer or soda was vastly preferable to the muddy looking, foul-tasting water which overwhelmed you with its chlorine content- both the smell and the taste.

Letters

I suspect that all soldiers are obsessive about letters from home and I remember how eager I was to get letters from home. The news from family members, friends and loved ones made it possible to continue to think about things other than the war. Some things stay the same. Reading Eugene's letters from a century before made clear not only his obsession with getting mail from home, but his difficulties and the expense to him in obtaining writing materials. His difficulties in buying expensive writing paper and stamps were mentioned as frequently as was his need to ask his family to send him items of clothing to supplement his army-issued uniforms or money to supplement his rations. Some soldiers in Vietnam sent and received cassette tapes of recorded conversations (oral letters) in place of written ones. Roger was one and he would get a package of tapes from home and then would spend hours in his area with his headphones on, listening to the sounds of home. Then later, he would spend equally long periods of time talking into a microphone recording his letters home.

August

It was considered bad luck to talk much about being a "short-timer," but after achieving that milestone, most soldiers started looking eagerly - almost obsessively - beyond the war and toward their departure. It is also interesting to note that in the following letter there is no reference to my injury (my leg was pretty much recovered by this time) as it no longer was the obsession that it had been only a few weeks earlier.

3 Aug 70
Hi,

I hope the license/registration got back quickly.

Things are going slowly here, which is nothing new. I had hoped to go on an R & R to Japan in a week or so - now it has been messed up & I can't go until the very end of the month. It makes a difference only in that there are a couple of things (one being to climb Mt. Fuji) which I may not be able to do after Aug. Very typical of the Army to mess up anything you could enjoy.

About Grandmothers house - no, I'm not interested in it. The dark room equipment is all movable. The very large plywood trays I would like to keep. The large tables - perhaps if there is room to put them, otherwise I shall build others. All the equipment - including the electric heater & the safe lite fixtures can be moved and stored in my studio or room. Sean can go through the stuff and decide what should be saved. It will be somewhat of a job as there is considerable junk. But there is no need to take down anything built in.

Would you please send me the latest bank statements from both Alfred & New York banks.

Also enclosed is a check (endorsed) from L. L. Bean for you to cash. (I bought some clothing for R & R from them!) Finally, enclosed is a check I would like certified - which I believe you can do without my being there - if not, just send me back the check or destroy it. Please send it back as soon as possible.

Also - I probably won't be sending you any money for a while preferring to wait until I get back to settle up debts. There is a problem of currency conversion (we don't get paid in U.S. Dollars but rather in MPC - military pay certificates),; there is a monthly limit on the amount of MPC which may be converted to U.S. Dollars. So about half my pay goes into a military savings account (which I cannot draw upon until I get back to the U.S.) and my checking account. So unless there is a real crisis I would prefer to wait until I return to settle my debts.

From the news about the atmosphere in N.Y.C. - I hope Betsy & Steve get up to Almond for a while!

Andy

The reference about the atmosphere in New York was to the increasingly polarized, ugly and emotionally charged atmosphere in the larger American cities. The opposition to, and divisiveness of, the Vietnam War had combined with the racial divisions created by the Civil Rights movement and caused an increasingly violent situation. Riots had become commonplace during the heat of the summer. The period of the late 1960's and early 70's is rightfully remembered as one of the periods in American history when great differences, which at times seemed almost unbridgeable, tested the nation. The divisions in American society were almost as deep as they had been before, during, and immediately after the Civil War. That August, New York City was shaken by great civil unrest and rioting - as were other cities, and much of the tension was centered on our involvement in Vietnam. In the Great Society gone bad, the riots in major American cities continued almost every summer from the mid 1960's until the early 1970's when we began to withdraw from Vietnam and its civil war and began to refocus our national priorities on solving our own internal problems.

The above letter contains a reference to my parents questions about whether I wanted my Grandmother's house and if not, then they had indicated that they wanted to clean it out and sell it. This reflected their conviction that my Grandmother would never return from Mobile, where she entered a nursing home following her fall and broken hip. Sadly, they were right and she did not ever leave the nursing home. I never saw her again. So my last memory of my Grandmother was that vision of her crying bitterly as I left for Vietnam.

Vietnam Funny Money - MPC

American bases pumped a huge amount of money into the local economy and so around them hastily built towns grew up very quickly. The burning of human excrement mentioned earlier was an assignment detested by GI's and so, when possible, was contracted out to Vietnamese civilians. Along with that onerous task, other more mundane ones - such as, picking up trash or cutting the brush, providing laundry service (mostly for officers or senior NCO's who could more easily afford it) or haircutting - were also jobbed out to local Vietnamese civilians when possible. (We often joked about the opportunity for intelligence gathering in these jobs and indeed, it was almost certainly true. The NVA and VC units certainly gathered a tremendous amount of intelligence this way. The American Army tried to be diligent in screening Vietnamese civilians to fill these jobs, but it more often relied on local authorities to do the hiring and screening of the workers.) The authorities tried a variety of ways to control the inflationary pressures this created - but without much success. Concerns multiplied about blackmarket trading as well with the result that an attempt was made to isolate the American soldiers from the Vietnamese civilian economy.

As a result, we were paid in Army script - Military Pay Coupons (MPC for short), referred to as play money, or Monopoly Money, since it resembled the phoney money of the board game. We also received monthly ration books for items like beer and cigarettes. Those of us who didn't smoke traded our cigarette coupons for other items and those who didn't drink did the same with beer or whiskey coupons. The script was only legal tender in base PX's - It was illegal for Vietnamese to own or use this script but it happened anyway. Script circulated like the legitimate currency it had become unofficially. Theoretically the "play money" could only be spent on base or at American PX's - but in fact, it was accepted everywhere. That created a thriving blackmarket and led to policies which tried to control the situation such as unannounced design changes in the MPC's or tight restrictions on how much money servicemen could send home. We also had to have some of our pay deposited in an account at home or in an army savings account.

We were paid regularly, but not a lot! My military pay voucher pay receipt for July 1970 showed my base pay was $231.60, with a foreign duty allowance of $13.00 and special pay (hazardous duty pay) of $65.00, for a grand total of $309.60, and, while I wasn't subject to withholding for income tax purposes, I was subject to Social Security withholding. Since I also had allocated withholding for a savings account and to purchase savings bonds my actual pay in "funny money" - MPC - was all of - $140!

Perfume River.

My R & R is in sight

As the end of August approached, the events of the summer and the flurry of activity in early July passed into memory. I began to think about the end of my tour.

My R & R - delayed but now very near - was the next big event in my year long odyssey:

> *22 Aug*
> *Hi*
>
> *A belated "Happy Birthday"! (By the time you get it!)* [My father's birthday was August 25.] *The past week or so has disappeared almost without my knowing it & I'm going to Japan on Wednesday.*
>
> *When I get back from Japan I will have just about 90 days (a few more) left here - time becoming a major preoccupation lately.*

I'm sure there must be hints of the changing seasons about now & even here the first signs of the oncoming Monsoon - the clouds; are now gathering & staying. All through May, June & July anything more than a brief (1/2 hr or so) rain storm was extremely rare & far between. The sky would be clear & cloudless for weeks. This week we have had 3 days of continuous rain & it has been cloudy the rest of the week.

At any rate the change in the weather has been a nice break.

Andy

Night Moon

Chapter 7   A "Shortimer"

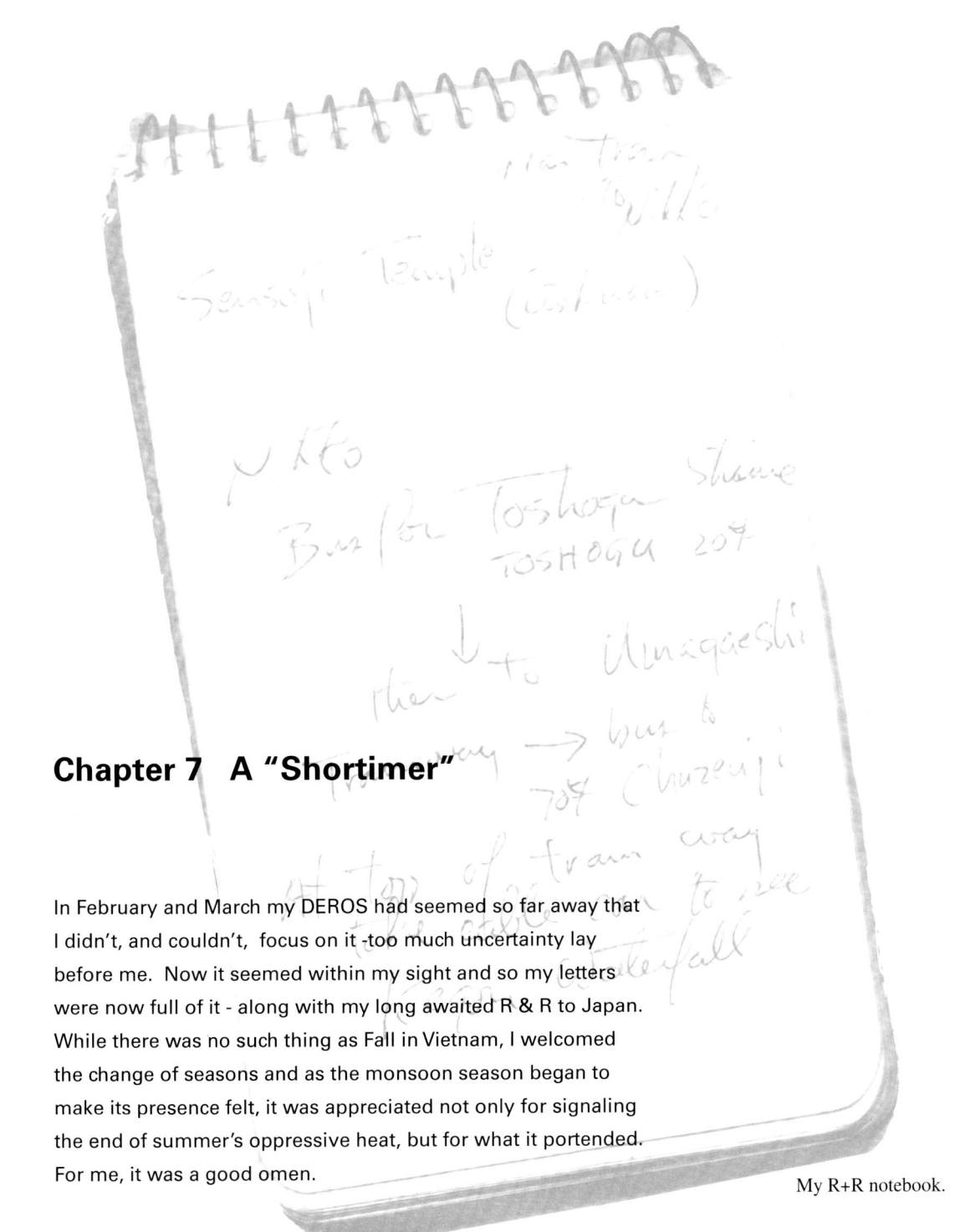

In February and March my DEROS had seemed so far away that I didn't, and couldn't, focus on it -too much uncertainty lay before me. Now it seemed within my sight and so my letters were now full of it - along with my long awaited R & R to Japan. While there was no such thing as Fall in Vietnam, I welcomed the change of seasons and as the monsoon season began to make its presence felt, it was appreciated not only for signaling the end of summer's oppressive heat, but for what it portended. For me, it was a good omen.

My R+R notebook.

Eugene's final months of service

Following a very brief stay near Washington, the 12th Maine was then sent to join the Army of the Shenandoah (the XIX Corps) under the direction of General Phil Sheridan. Sheridan's orders were simple: proceed to the Shenandoah Valley, flush out the confederates under Jubal Early, drive them south and destroy anything that could not be used. Sheridan, true to his reputation, drove his men hard.

In August of 1864, Eugene's diary records marches begun in the middle of the night, often at 1 AM and continuing until noon the following day. Some days they marched all night:

Tuesday, August 16, 1864 Started at 1 o'clock again. Have forded Goose Creek and are now camped near Leesburg. We have marched about 8 miles.

Wednesday 17. Started at 3 o'clock this morning and marched 16 miles and camped but we have got orders again now and to start again. We are within a mile of Snickers Gap. I have had a good nap today and I needed it much.

The R & R

Every GI, enlisted or officer, who served in Vietnam was entitled to one week of Rest & Relaxation (an R & R) - in short, a vacation - after serving in country for more than 6 months. Unlike World War II where troops, as units, were rotated out of combat (and replaced with other units) on a regular basis for rest, in Vietnam, units could not be rotated out but individuals could! This focus on the individual as needing an R & R was consistent with the concept of using individual replacements for replenishment rather than the unit replacement system that the Army utilized during the Second World War.) Out of this belief that giving the troops a rest would help improve the morale of troops, was born the concept of an R & R. It was unique, and as Ronald Spector wrote in his book, *After Tet*: *"Of the hundreds of special military projects and programs the Americans introduced in Vietnam, R & R was one of the few unalloyed successes. It was also one of the most improbable. That thousands of American GI's in their early twenties could be airlifted from the jungles and rice paddies of Vietnam to a large Asian city, left to their own devices for five or six days and then returned to their duties in Vietnam without serious incident seemed so unlikely that only the actual record of success over more than six years could have proven otherwise. "* (After Tet, pg 270)

You were authorized to take this R & R in any locations where the U.S. had established R & R centers. These were, as I recall: Hawaii (If you were married, your wife could meet you there.), Bangkok, Manila, Singapore, Kuala Lumpur, Taipei, Hong Kong, Sidney and Tokyo. After the dates and place of your request were approved, the Air Force would fly you to one of the R & R centers where you could stay - or, in several of the countries, where you could travel on your own, arranging your own seven day vacation. Each of the countries and centers offered a different kind of experience.

Short of your DEROS, the date of your scheduled R & R was the event most dreamed about, thought about and talked about by GI's in the Army - particularly those in combat units living under extremely difficult conditions. For many GI's, it was a time to engage in some previously unimaginable adventures - while leaving the war behind for a week. For some, it was a week of carnal pleasure, for others it was a time of nonstop shopping or it was a time to spend a week on a beach, or seeing tourist sights. Except for those men meeting wives in Hawaii, each of us thought about the choices endlessly. We listened to the stories and reports of those who went and returned, looking carefully at their pictures and asking many, many questions. All of us daydreamed about the week of R & R because it was escapist thinking - it gave us something other than the war to think about. Some of us researched the possible sites, reading literature or asking family or friends to send us guide books on our top preferences. But we finally chose our own R & R very carefully. The debates over the best location were frequent and often heated. Once you returned, the bragging rights over who had the best R & R were fiercely defended.

I chose to travel to Japan, a country I had always been fascinated with, but one I never expected to see. I couldn't resist the chance to visit there. Japan also offered GI's a chance to travel within the country as opposed to staying in an Army R & R Center. I wanted to do that; I didn't want to be with other soldiers on my R & R - my idea was to leave the war and soldiers behind and not to think about the war for a week.

The plan

187

Thursday, August 18, 1864. We crossed the Blue Ridge last night just before dark and then forded the Shenandoah River. They put our Regt. in advance and I suppose they expected trouble after crossing the river. We marched about 8 miles marching a good part of the night. We stopped a short time [in] Berryville and caught up with Sheridan's army. We started again this morning and have marched about eight miles and are now resting in woods on the road to Harper's Ferry. Sheridan is falling back. It rained hard part of today and our men are pretty well played out.
(Vintage, pg. 301)

Today, thousands of cars pour over Snickers Gap on the Berryville Pike (Highway 7), but when Eugene marched over it, it was a steeply winding road that must have challenged his stamina.

By the 21st, there was fighting all around and Eugene's regiment was in some skirmishing. By Tuesday, the 23rd he begins to feel unwell:
Wednesday August 24   I had a pretty hard shake today.
Thursday 25 I am not very well and it continues to get worse.

I arrived in Japan for my long awaited R & R on August 27, 1970. My notebook plans read:

 27 Thur - Arrive
 28 Fri   - Tokyo/night
 29 Sat   - Nikko
 30 Sun - Hakone-Yumoto
 31 Mon - Shimoda
 1   Tues - Izu Peninsula
 2   Wed - Tokyo/night
 3   Thur - Leave

And then - a reminder:
 R R Reporting date 3 Sept. 10:30 -12:00 Camp Zama R & R Center)

Long before I actually left, I spent hours poring over guidebooks and doing endless planning. I had decided to spend a couple of days in Tokyo and then go to Nikko, back through Tokyo to Hakone-Yumoto and Shimoda (the area around Mt. Fuji) and then on to the Izu Peninsula before returning to the Tokyo R & R center and back to Vietnam. It almost worked that way although I spent one absolutely delightful, and completely unplanned, night in a ryokan (a traditional Japanese inn) in the village near the temple complex at Nikko. And, while I planned to climb Mt. Fuji, the threat of a typhoon kept me from going up, and so, instead, I spent that day touring the lakes and countryside around the base of the mountain - which was very, very beautiful and probably more enjoyable.

When I flew out of Vietnam for Tokyo, I had been in Vietnam for more than 8 months, and when I returned, I would truly be a "short timer". On that day of departure for Tokyo, I left the Aviation Group in the morning carrying a few civilian clothes and a camera and caught a ride on a Huey down to Da Nang. Once there, I easily found my way to the R & R processing Center.

The Da Nang R & R processing center was set up to handle GI's from all over the northern tier of Vietnam (I Corps) who were departing on their R & R. There, you were given time to shower and clean up and buy some civilian items of clothing in the PX. Soldiers who arrived with only the uniform they were wearing - and many did -were able to buy clothes and other civilian necessities that they had left "back in the world". For many, including myself, that included a suitcase and some chinos and civilian shirts.   My military passenger jet left Da Nang, and in a couple of hours we landed at a US base just outside Tokyo from which we were taken to the Camp Zama R & R Center. On the plane I sat next to an older sergeant, "a lifer" who had been in Vietnam on several tours of duty. He had previously served in Japan for a few years and knew many people in the Tokyo area. His idea of an ideal R & R was to shack up with a woman he knew for the week and he urged me to do the same, saying that he was certain he could arrange it for me. While it sounded wonderful in some ways, I thought that I would probably never get back to Japan and so I thanked him, but said I really wanted to travel and see what I could of Japan during the short time I had. However, I did take one of his suggestions and spent my first night at a hotel that catered to GI's instead of staying at the Army's R & R Center on the US Army base.

The next day I took the fabled Tokyo subway to Ueno Park, where I wandered in wonder looking at some magnificant temples - the Kiyomizu do, and the Toshu gu as well as the Ueno Zoo. I also went to the National Museum of Western Art (designed by Le Corbusier) adjacent to the park. (But I didn't

Saturday, August 27, This morning I was sent to the hospital by the doctor. I am at Sandy Hook about a mile from Harpers's Freey. I have had a chill today.

He is evacuated by rail to the U.S. General Hospital in Frederick City, Maryland on the 29th of August and disingenuously writes his mother:
Dear Mother,

It has been some time since I wrote, and perhaps you are getting uneasy but you need not if you do not hear very often, for I cannot get a chance to write every day. You will see by the date of this that I am now in the hospital. I am not very sick, only down with the Fever and Argue which is nothing alarming and I am better off that I came here three days ago from Harper's Ferry where I left my Regt. after leaving Tennally Town...

I hope this will reach you for it is the last envelope, sheet of paper or postage stamp I have got. I hope, however, that I shall not have to write many more letters befor having the joy of seeing you all...
(Vintage, pgs. 302 and 303)

try to explore it - the Museum was huge.) Ueno Park was lovely and it was a magical experience simply to wander among peaceful people who were out for an afternoon stroll in the park. It was an incredibly wonderful experience just to sit on a park bench for half an hour and soak up the sense of peace and normalcy - to watch families strolling in a modern city much like New York, a place that seemed centuries from the dust, dirt, smells and ever present sense of danger in Vietnam.

The next day, in overcast and misty weather, I took a sleek fast train north to the ancient (and huge) temple complex at Nikko, leaving most of my luggage at the hotel and carrying only a small bag with my camera equipment, a change of clothes and

A temple complex at Nikko

a lightweight nylon windbreaker that I thought was water repellent - but very quickly learned was only minimally water resistent . After alighting from the train, I headed up the main street which was filled with shops, toward the temple complex located some distance away. I explored several of the side streets and there I discovered a couple of wonderful antique

Another view of Nikko

shops full of an incredible array of art and antiquities. Scrolls and paintings, bronzes and ceramics and furniture were everywhere. I took a very cursory look at things and decided that I would stop for serious shopping on my way back to the train.

The temple complex in Nikko is huge, with the temples and shrines covering acres of meadows and wooded glades up in the mountains north of Tokyo, near a lake which is part of Nikko Park, a beautiful nature reserve. When I arrived (late in the morning) the lake was still partially covered in mist as I walked past on the way to the temple complex. During all the hours I spent there in Nikko, all memories of the war disappeared and I became immersed in a magical place surrounded by the beauty and majesty of the ancient complex. After leaving the lake, one entered a world of green, with bright sunlight filtering through mostly old, tall and stately trees. A very gentle breeze would rustle the leaves of the trees, and, when it wasn't raining, the sun was warm, but not oven-hot as it was in Vietnam. (While it had briefly rained in Vietnam before I left, it was still brutally hot at the end of the dry summer season, the sun still baking and the red dust overwhelming.)

Part of the main shrine at Nikko, the Tosho gu, contains the famous panel of the three monkeys "hear no evil, see no evil and speak no evil". But they are only part of the vast cornucopia of visual richness that is there. After spending the day in the temple complex, wandering from temple to temple under a canopy of majestic trees and feeling like I was in a magical kingdom, I was unable to tear myself away in time to catch a train back to Tokyo, and lingered late in the day. When the drizzle turned to rain and my windbreaker turned out to be less than water repellent, I went looking for a place to stay. I found a modest traditional Japanese inn, a ryokan which turned out to be wonderful. A typical Japanese hot bath followed by a modest and delightfully simple dinner restored me. It was a long way from Camp Eagle and Thua Thien Province.

A view from Shimoda

The next day, I returned to one of the wonderful antique shops that I had spotted on my way from the station to the temple complex and spent hours agonizing over possible purchases. I looked at numerous items and, not being able to easily choose from such a profusion of treasures, agonized repeatedly over the choices, asking the owner (who was very patient with me) to show me things several times so I could compare them. I could have spent all my money in that shop in no time but I tried hard to stay within a self-imposed budget so as not to spend all my limited funds at the beginning of my R & R. My efforts were without complete success and I spent about twice what I planned. I finally settled on an 18th-Century Chinese scroll of a nobleman (complete with certificate of authenticity and a translation of the Chinese poem into Japanese), a wonderful 19th- Century woodblock triptych, and an 18th-Century woodblock plus a couple of relatively small 19th-Century woodblock prints (very small but very good) and a Japanese hand bell. All were carefully wrapped (the scroll came in its own beautifully made wooden box) and placed in my bag, and I very reluctantly went back to the station to take the train to Tokyo where I left my purchases safely stored with my luggage in the hotel where I planned to spend my last night. Then I headed south by train (a local) toward Hakone and Shimoda where I planned to climb Mt. Fuji.

Unfortunately, no one was permitted to go up Mt. Fuji since a Typhoon was due in, and indeed, the next few days continued rainy and windy. The weather didn't detract from my enjoyment - or slow down my travel. I traveled through the area around Mt. Fuji and experienced some of the most wonderful days in my life. This area around Mt. Fuji is often referred to as the Japanese Alps. It is an area of wonderfully wild terrain with spectacular scenery. I rode a modern boat disguised to look like a pirate ship across Lake Ashino, rode a cable car

Another page from the notebook.

across picturesque valleys, traveling as well by foot and bus, finally ending in Atami where I found a ryokan for the evening. The plan was to catch a train the next day down to Shimoda.

An entry from my notebook dated August 30 reads:

A coffee house in Hakone-Yumoto where I have a quart of beer & some salted nuts in front of me - 230 yen or less than 75 cents. (At the then current exchange rate ....)

Very good dinner music playing. Very quiet & peaceful - very far from the war I shall go back to: hard to believe they exist so close together. One of the incongruities of VN of course has been the fact that one goes off to war with peace all around him.

The bar (coffee shop) decor is bastard Western - complete with plastic plants & West Side Story on the piped in music (as the mood music!)

All this in the shadow of Mt. Fuji & the lush South Japanese Alps!!

And then - referring to another selection of music: *"In English a choral version of A Man and A Woman."*

The Izu Peninsula juts out beyond the lower area of Tokyo Bay, and it, too, is a rocky and wild place but incredibly is really within a short distance of the Tokyo/Yokohama urban metropolitan area. Shimoda, a small city (when I visited it) was situated at the eastern end of that rugged peninsula. This is the eastern most

Fishing boats near Shimoda

spot in Japan and was enshrined in Japanese history as the spot where Admiral Perry first landed in Japan in 1853. In 1970 the only easy way to Shimoda was via rail, on a small, narrow gauge railroad that wound its way along the shore of the peninsula. It was a scenic ride following the shoreline giving one a breathtaking view of Tokyo Bay. In Shimoda, I wandered through the town, sat on some huge rocks above the Pacific, watched breaking waves and looked toward California, wondering what it must have been like for the first Americans of Commodore Perry's fleet when they landed. I thought of the Japanese who upon first seeing those Americans must have thought them very strange people. The fleets of beautifully decorated boats below me made me wonder if boats such as those sailed out to meet Perry.

In a coffee shop there, I spent a hour talking with a Japanese man who wondered what my life was like in Vietnam and why America was fighting there. He asked what America thought it would or could accomplish in the war there.
I couldn't provide many insights!

From Shimoda I took the train back to Tokyo and spent one last night there. On the bus to the airport the following day, I sat next to the same sergeant I had met on the flight in. He looked rested and said he had a wonderful time. As expected, he had been pampered and had thoroughly enjoyed the stay. I said I had a wonderful time traveling but that I was very

My pirate ship on Lake Ashino

On September 9, he got his discharge from the hospital and rejoined his regiment in Harper's Ferry:

Saturday 10 We had a day's rations issued today and started for the front. We stop at Charleston tonight in an old church.

Sunday, September 11, 1864. We had a heavy shower last night and made it muddy walking today but I have reached the Regt. near Berryville. I am not very tired.

But on Sunday the 18th he would write: *Inspection this morning and I had a severe chill after it. I fear they are coming on to me full force.*

Monday, September 19, 1864   We moved at two o'clock this morning and marched near Winchester where we had a bloody battle. I had another touch of the shakes and was only in the first part of it and I do not know how many were killed in our company, but I hear they suffered heavily. (Vintage, pgs, 304, 305 and 309)

This was the battle of Winchester. He had little more than six weeks remaining on his enlistment.

tired. I slept all the way back to Da Nang where I changed into my old jungle fatigues and boots and then I caught a helicopter back to Camp Eagle carefully carrying my purchases - and treasuring my memories.

On the whole Japan trip, I made no reservations except for the first and last nights. For the other nights, I would begin looking for a ryokan after a day filled with countless pleasures. Some days, I would have to visit many ryokans before I found one toward evening, and on a couple of nights it was quite late in the evening before I found one. But each was clean, had very simple rooms, the staff provided faultless service and of course, each had a wonderful hot bath and a clean futon.

I liked Japanese food (which I had never had before) from the beginning. To conserve my small budget I almost always ate in small modest shops which posted their menu and prices along with a plastic facsimile of each dish in the window . Since my Japanese was limited to a very few phrases, I could always take the waiter or waitress to the display case and point to my selection. My tastes were simple: the Japanese beer was heavenly, as were the prawns and fish dishes with rice and vegetables. I was very happy.

My letter to my parents expressed my feelings well :

> *Have received a multitude of books - am esp. Pleased with the Nabokov, Grass & Durrell. In fact excited about reading them!*
>
> *My trip to Japan was great even though it rained most of the time & I didn't get a chance to climb Mt. Fuji!*
>
> *I went to Nikko, Hakone-Yumoto, Shimoda, Ito & another small town on the Izu Peninsula (Atagawa).*

Only stayed in Tokyo one day - its much like NYC & none too pleasant in late summer (I.e. Replete with dirt, fumes, heat, etc.) I packed a small (camera) bag with my camera & a change of clothes & took off leaving my suitcase in Tokyo. I stayed where I could nights; in Ryokans (Japanese style inns) always - never making a reservation. Some nights I had to stop at 8-10 ryokans before finding one that would take me - we would agree upon a price thru gestures & a few words of English - or in a couple of cases, thru gestures alone.

I almost never saw another European or American & when I did, I promptly went the other way. I ate, of course, Japanese food (which I like very much). A side benefit was the beer - Japanese beer is great!

Traveling by train in Japan (2nd Class) is extraordinarily cheap & delightful.

I did take pictures - though not too many - often I felt I would offend & often I felt more like looking & enjoying rather than photographing.

I stumbled across a couple of antique shops (by accident) & thereby acquired a number of prints & one very fine hanging (Chinese - & quite expensive; also complete with Japanese translation! Listed in a trade manual!) It shall arrive shortly via registered air mail. Also one bronze bell which shall remain here & be hand carried back (or shipped later) & one tea cup - a gift from the woman at one of the shops - apparently I charmed her with my appreciation of what she had in her shop (My God -to have had $500 to spend!) - it shall also stay here temp.

Some of the prints are so-so (but nice) & some are excellent. Range in price from .30 to $30 (The hanging scroll not a print.) Very hard to find - if *possible even - in the US.*

Will give some as gifts & some to be kept. Will label.

All are very fragile so handle with care.

Thanks for the bank statement - when I originally set up the thing the money was to go into my Savings account. But when it went into my checking account I decided that was just as good. It doesn't matter - just so I know where (which account) its going into so I don't write a check that bounces! Keep sending the statements (checking particularly.) Did you find out to whom I apply for an absentee ballot - I asked in my last letter to Sean?!

Have been trying to finish this letter for 3 days now - we are in the throes of an epidemic of dysentery & our dispensary is not only understaffed now but also hit by the epidemic so those of us still healthy are working like hell.

Please check into that Absentee Ballot for me - I would like to vote this fall.

Andy

As the next to last paragraph indicated - coming back to Vietnam was to return to earth with a thud. The dispensary was very busy with the epidemic of dysentery, and, since several of the medics had left either while I was in Japan or shortly after I got back, we were very short-handed.

Shortimer

Like many other soldiers, as I got closer to my DEROS date, I began to indulge myself from the PX catalog and spend some of the money I had been saving on electronic equipment that I then had sent home:

29 Sept.

Thanks for the letters. Before I forget - a "thank you" for the desk which I'm looking forward to seeing.
By the way - I didn't mean to make the prints & scroll sound so fragile but over here they seemed extremely so! And I was really excited about finding them! Also before I forget I should warn Dad that there will be arriving (when I don't know) some stereo equipment which I am in the process of getting - & having sent home addressed to him!
There may be some duty on a couple of them $15-$20. Hopefully I shall send some cash home to cover it - but the conversion problem may prevent it. However, rest assured I shall (sometime) pay you - also they are addressed to you as a matter of conve-

General Wright arriving at Boy Scout Jamboree

nience (rather than having it addressed to me c/o you.)

Also my thanks for paying the taxes on my land. When I get back I should have ample money to pay my bills...unless someone puts another engine in the Ford! (After I finish paying bills I probably won't be much ahead but what the hell!)

At any rate expect four packages (1 receiver, 1 tape deck, 2 speakers) sometime in the next 1-4 months (I have no idea how long it will take!) Perhaps not till I get there.

I have about 70 days left!

The rains have started - every evening about 6 PM it begins raining & continues till the middle of the night. Shortly it shall be raining continually. Last year (in Oct), a record year, they got 22" of rain in 24 hrs!

I should get some of my (rather poor) photo's of Japan labeled & sent on within a week or so. Some of them anyway.

We have a couple of new medics in so we aren't quite as short handed now.

Andy

Not only was I a "short-timer," but as the letter indicated, things had changed with the dispensary. Most of the medics that I had worked with for much of my tour had already left. Jim had gone in early summer as had Jaster and Royce. Dr. R went home in August, Randy left when I was in Japan, Dave left shortly after I got back from my R & R, Charlie, Roger, Bruce and I were the only remaining medics from the group that had spent much of the year together. Charlie, Roger and Bruce had each decided (but for very different reasons) that they would extend their Vietnam duty and so they were looking at six more months. I had decided not to extend (also for a number of reasons) and I now had the shortest time left on my tour of duty of the four remaining medics who had worked together for so long. There was no doctor in residence.

During mid-September, I spent one very pleasant day working as a driver and photographer for Major G, one of our "Loach" pilots. He was participating in a Vietnamese Boy Scout ceremony and wanted someone to document the event and his participation in it. The colorful ceremony took place in the Citadel in Hue and was very touching, and also very surreal, filled as it was with American-style Scout rituals amid the ruins of war. It was attended by a number of military and civilian dignitaries, including our former commanding General, John M. Wright, by then the Commanding general of MACV in I Corps. I felt like I was in a time warp: here we were in a war and here we were at a Scout jamboree, an encampment with Vietnamese children all dressed up in their Scouting Uniforms looking like they could have stepped out of the Sunday magazine section from the local newspaper in almost any part of the United States. It was almost as odd as was flying to Vietnam on the flight with miniskirted stewardesses. (Perhaps more so.)

Boy Scouts playing game while blindfolded

The downside of the new arrivals was that the close working relationship of medics at the dispensary which had been forged during those many months of working together as a team, all but disappeared. The new arrivals didn't seem to mesh well with those of us who remained. The first of the new arrivals was an Sp/7 replacement for Dave and he quickly showed he was the worst kind of "lifer" (derogatory term for a regular army career soldier) because he took one look at the way the dispensary was functioning and said (in effect) "keep up the good work" and made himself as invisible as possible, preferring to spend his time at the NCO Club where they served cold beer rather than contributing to the work at the dispensary. With Dr. R gone, for all practical purposes we were now without a well trained medical specialist as well!

Since I was getting "short" (I didn't know how short at the time) I began to do what all shorttimers did, just kept my head down and did only what was needed - no more volunteering for anything. I began to get very superstitious - the evenings I had duty in the dispensary were the worst, because we had been hit so often on either the night I was on duty - or the night afterwards! And, when we were short handed, it meant that I was on duty every third or fourth night.

Toward the end of the summer we began hearing rumors that, in order to begin the troop reductions and meet the target levels that President Nixon had promised, some Army personnel would get early DEROS dates. In September, after I got back from Japan, several soldiers I knew received "drops" and left Vietnam before their DEROS dates. I wrote home in early October:

Girl Scouts

Hi,

Just a brief note to say hello & pass on some news and ask for some.

First, I've shipped home some books & will be shipping more. Also will send on a few other things. Have received notice that my stereo-receiver was shipped from PACEX so that probably will arrive home before I do! Its addressed to Mr. LL Phelan & there will be some duty due (about $13) which I will send you shortly after the beginning of next month.

I know I also have life insurance & car insurance due in October though I believe I have a 30 day grace period on the life. Please let me know what my Alfred Checking Balance is.

Also please get a few warm clothes; sweater, pair of pants, etc together & send them to NYC. There is a chance I may be getting back in the States before I am scheduled to. So called 'Drops' are beginning to appear (this is when someone leaves RVN before his full year is up - before his normal DEROS) people are now getting 5-12 day drops & the rumor has them extending on into Dec. I'm not counting on it but it appears likely that the rumor is true.

At any rate - I am getting ready to leave & plan to be ready to leave on very short notice after the 1st of Nov. That is; I'm beginning to pack things, etc.

Betsy & Steve have said they will be going to Chicago for D. J's wedding at Thanksgiving so if I get back in the U.S. about then I'm not sure whether I will fly into NYC or not. Will have to wait until I hear from Harriet.

You should have received the slides (from Japan) by now.

By the way, the article on Japanese 'Ryokans'

> *exaggerates a bit - perhaps the more expensive ones are romantic & luxurious as the article says but the ones I stayed at were quite simple though exquisite & very comfortable. I did not have (ever) a room with private bath but the "public" one in the ryokan was more than adequate. There was however, always tea awaiting me in my room.*
>
> *Things here are going on in a routine manner - I'm afraid I try to think as little about them as possible.*
>
> *Andy*

In late October the "drops" hit me in a bigger way than I ever imagined! In a brief note masking my excitement, I sent home the news to my parents:

> *26 Oct*
>
> *Well its official - I leave Vietnam on Nov 10 (25 days early).*
>
> *Should get into NY by the 11th or 12th (& I do plan to go there unless I hear to the contrary from B & S!)*
>
> *At any rate - no more mail to this address!*
>
> *Andy*

I wrote one final letter to Betsy and Steve which had a bit more information since I was trying to arrange some social activity upon my return :

Hi,

A brief note to let you know I shall be in NYC on the 11th or 12th of Nov.

I asked Harriet to spend a few days with me at your place (I hope I didn't presume too much). However since I got a letter from her tonight (first time in two months) which is ambiguous to say the least (& which implies she might be glad to see me - if she can manage the time!? I doubt I shall see her - or barely)

At any rate - Susan P. is still (I think) in the NYC area (was a few weeks ago - but knowing her!?) & if Harriet is as her letter sounds, I may ask Susan to come down! I don't know what the deal is with Harriet but must be I presumed too much.

But what ever the circumstances I shall appear on your doorstep sometime after the 10th.

Andy

The comment about the letter from Harriet made it clear that I was pretty certain she had moved on. My other comments made it clear that I wasn't going to pine over it. So , alerted to the trials and travails of the "real world, " I made preparations to reenter it. Whatever awaited me, I was delighted about the early departure date and the next couple of weeks became a blur - partially because I was processing out, thinking of the trip home and I was still busy with things in the dispensary, pulling normal duty hours including night duty - although Charlie volunteered to take my last scheduled patrol.

Now that I was one of the lucky ones getting a 25-day drop and leaving early, I began to have conflicting feelings, joy at leaving early and going back to the world, but also sadness. The dispensary, a little tin and plywood shack surrounded by a sea of sandbags in a dirty dusty war-scarred spot in Vietnam had been my home for the past 11 plus months, and I had worked closely with those men during that time. While there was no sentimental attachment to the place, there was, because of shared experiences, a bond with that place. A feeling of belonging to the dispensary had developed in me. And so, contrary to every impulse in my body and completely contradicting that letter I had written so many months earlier, I began to feel sad at leaving those friends who had shared so many experiences with me and who collectively had managed to run a decent operation in an indecent war.

Chapter 8
Return to the World

My orders for reassignment directed me to the 595th MD Medical Co, in Ft. Devens, Massachusetts and I had about two weeks to prepare to leave the Division. The time was used to get through my outprocessing from the 101st Avn group and the Division. The Army was skilled in moving men around and so it moved quickly to get one from the field in Vietnam back to the US once the orders were cut. But it also meant a lot of paper work. I had to get authorizations from various levels of the Army, starting with my company, and I also needed to get medical clearance which was easy - I signed myself off (we still didn't have a doctor in the dispensary) ! While we were authorized to ship a certain amount of personal baggage back home from Vietnam, I simply gave away or threw out most of my unofficial "stuff" such as most of my books, assorted accumulations of scrounged clothing and other personal belongings. I passed on the liberated 45 Colt pistol that had been bequeathed to me by Jaster and ended up packing and shipping only a small number of things -mostly issued items, but a few things like my radio. I tried to carry with me a minimal amount - only what I would need on my trip.

On my departure date from the 101st Aviation Group, I caught a ride on a Huey to DaNang where, as I recall (that period of time was a blur), I was debriefed, received the decorations I had been awarded, then was processed out of MACV (the Vietnam theater of operations), and given new orders officially authorizing my transportation stateside. In the afternoon, I was scheduled to catch a flight down to Cam Ranh Bay - on a 20-25 year old C-47! On the first takeoff try in a pouring rainstorm, the pilot aborted because oil was spewing from one of the engines.

Eugene's last few weeks

Eugene's diary entries after the Battle of Winchester were hard for me to read. He was within 60 days of the end of his three year enlistment.

"Tuesday 20 I came off the wagon train and caught up with the Regt. They were near Strasburg. I had an awful shake coming up. Our Company has only 13 men present now. Our Captain is killed. Two corporals wounded, 3 privates wounded, one mortally, 2 sergeants and 8 men missing.

Wednesday, September 21, 1864. Today one man came in and said that he buried Sergeant Berry and private Herr. Sergeant Pashey is missing. We moved this morning and went west into the brow of a hill and had orders to pitch tents, but before...we had orders to strike again and are now waiting orders. I am about played out. (Vintage, pg. 310)

Sheridan set out in pursuit of Early and the 12th Maine marched as far south as Harrisonburg, but they lost contact with Early's army. Then they began to destroy the farms and livestock as they marched up and down the Shenandoah Valley.

That was not a good sign and it was definitely something that needed fixing! We deplaned and impatiently waited for hours while the mechanics worked on the plane but then the monsoon rains settled in and prevented another try that night. Informed that we would try again in the morning, I spent my last night in Vietnam, cold and damp, but trying to get comfortable in a dreary seahut next to the DaNang runway. Using our duffle bags as pillows with our field jackets pulled over us, we stretched out on the floor and struggled to sleep but we were all fitful and impatient for dawn. Late that night there were a few incoming rounds and, although it was far away from us, I cursed them anyway.

Shortly after dawn the plane took off safely without incident and we arrived in Cam Ranh Bay about an hour later where, since we had missed our scheduled flight out of Vietnam, we had to wait for the next available flight which wasn't until the middle of the night. We spent the day impatiently waiting - either reading or sleeping or talking aimlessly (mostly about what we would do when we got back). Finally, under a moonlit sky with the heat still radiating off the beautiful white sand, the charter jet that would take us back to the US landed. When that plane came in and taxied to a halt, we all cheered - all of us looking sunburned and scruffy in worn and faded jungle fatigues as the replacement troops coming off the plane in their clean new uniforms, struggling to carry their heavy duffle bags across the tamarac toward the terminal, gave us wary glances. I'm sure that everyone standing there cheering remembered that day the previous year, when we were the ones struggling across the tamarac in our clean new uniforms and the waiting soldiers, looking as dirty and scruffy as we now did, cheered our arrival! We were taking their seats on the flight out, and we were just as happy as those who had watched us a year earlier had been.

The speed of processing when we landed in the US at McChord AFB was really amazing. My travel voucher from the trip back shows that I left Cam Ranh Bay at I AM on November 12, 1970 and, with a stop in Yokota, Japan arrived in McChord Air Force Base in Washington State, then departed for processing at nearby Ft. Lewis where we arrived at 3 AM. There I received a new dress green uniform, clean underwear, had time to shower and shave, and received another short debriefing which was a lecture on how to behave back in the world. Telephones were available, so many of us called home or talked to loved ones to indicate that we were safely back "in the world". We had time for a meal and then we were issued our new "dress greens" which allowed us, for the first time, to wear our campaign ribbons and medals. Then we were bused back to the Seattle Airport where I had a seat on a commercial flight for New York's Kennedy Airport landing at 11 PM East Coast time - still on the 12th of November! My trip back to the world - from the sands of Cam Ranh Bay in Vietnam to a SoHo loft in New York City - was complete in the same day! (Of course it lasted longer than 24 hours since I regained the day I had lost when I went to Vietnam.)

One of the things I remember vividly was how nervous I was on the bus ride from McChord Air Force Base to Ft. Lewis when I realized that there was no one providing an armed escort. I also remember the New York cab driver's kindness and concern when he dropped me off in the middle of the night on Greene Street (in SoHo) at Betsy and Steve's loft. It was still long before it was fashionable for anyone to live there in those loft spaces, and most were still used for light manufacturing. In fact, living there wasn't even legal in 1970. The driver and I talked a lot on the ride in from Kennedy (he had nephews in Vietnam) and he was very nice, and very concerned about my

Friday, October 7, 1864 We have done some hard marching today. We are camped now about 2 miles from Woodstock. We have forded 3 streams and marched about 20 miles. Did not get into camp until long after dark. We burn all the barns.
(Vintage, pg. 315)

They stayed in camp at Cedar Creek for the next 6 days. Then on the early morning of the 19th, the decisive battle of Cedar Creek occurred. Eugene's letter home on the 24th:

...That morning, the 19th, just a month from the fight at Winchester. Our brigade was routed out about 3 o'clock to go on a reconnaissance and we had just got through breakfast when the Rebs stole a march on us and surprised the 8th corps in their camps....Soon the bullets and shell began to come our way and then, too late to form a line, it was found that the Rebs had carried the works on our left and that we were ouflanked...We fell back steadily, halting and firing upon them when we got the chance, while the 8th cops ran like frightened sheep. We fell back to the 6th corps and then the fight was kept up with no stop until about noon

without much advantage on either side. Then old Sheridan came up from Winchester where he had heard of the fight and he was "awful raving" and swore like a pirate and said that he would show them a game that would be worth two of theirs, and he did, out flanking them and we drove them into nothing....In the afternoon I sprained my ankle slightly and was unable to reach the Regt. that night...Mell Gould was with me, and we camped out on the field among the dead and wounded....The dead and wounded Rebs were strewn all along the road where they had been left in their flight...
(Vintage, pgs. 322-323)

This was the decisive battle of the Shenandoah campaign. Early's army was no longer a threat to Sheridan. It was also Eugene's last battle.

destination. He thought I had an incorrect address and so he waited until the door opened.

The World

I was dropped back into "the world" with a thud - no soft reentry for me. It really was another, almost alien world and there were many things that took some getting used to - the traffic and the crowds of people. I had changed and the city had changed since I had last been there the year before. Something very insignificant sticks in my mind and that was how shocked I was to see long hair and beards or mustaches on the NYC cops. (While I was away, the patrolmen's association had won the right for patrolmen to wear their hair long after years of having to wear very short military style haircuts. I was seeing it for the first time.)

I was immediately and completely immersed in a world full of social life with crowded loft parties, and late evenings at places like the Spring Street Bar, where I was overwhelmed. New York was so different from Vietnam in its sights, smells, and noises. Instead of rice paddies and red dusty roads with water buffalo, motor bikes, trucks and jeeps, with helicopters clattering overhead, there were subways and crowds of well dressed people dashing to and fro in the shadows of the skyscrapers and tall buildings with police and fire sirens at night replacing the sounds of incoming and outgoing rounds. Instead of baggy olive drab uniforms and black pajamas, people dressed in fashionably different colors, styles and ways. You came and went when you wanted. You hailed a cab and went where you wanted to go or you walked all over the city. It was an unbelievable change from my existence in Vietnam to be in a city environment that included such freedom.

I stayed for the next few days in NYC with my sister and her husband Steve in their loft in SoHo. They were part of the SoHo art community, and almost all of the Soho community detested the war in Vietnam and all were enjoying a creative and unstructured, richly alternative and nonconforming, bohemian life-style that contrasted dramatically with the tightly focused rigidly hierarchal army existence I had been living under. Needless to say they were neither sympathetic to the war, nor towards my experiences - which made little impression on them. For them, living in the physical confines of the city, and in the intensely creative and introspective world of SoHo, Vietnam was an abstract concept completely incomprehensible to them as it was utterly removed from their experience and understanding of any reality. I felt as if I had inhabited an alien world for the past year and my Vietnam experience really seemed to belong to another world. Except when I was with a couple of close friends who asked specifically, I stopped talking about it. I had a very good time, but after a week, I went to Almond to see my parents and spend Thanksgiving with them.

When my parents met me as I got off the plane in Elmira, my father remarked, somewhat to my surprise, that he thought I would be wearing my uniform. But after my time in New York, I knew better than that; I knew that even mentioning I had been in Vietnam, let alone wearing an Army uniform in those days was asking to become the center of a great deal of unwanted attention and a lot of it could be abusive.

It was cold and snowy in Almond, and I was not used to that at all. I shivered and I couldn't get warm. Thanksgiving had always been a cherished ritual with my family and that year was much more wonderful than usual. The day included a large dinner with family and family friends who had all celebrated the holiday together for years. I had not expected to spend this

211

Thanksgiving with them, so it was a very, very special day. But I also realized things had changed. My Grandmother no longer sat at the table on my father's left side where she could have her sherry glass easily refilled.

It was great to be home and I enjoyed being in the house, and in the town where I grew up, sleeping late, visiting with family and friends and feeling relaxed. I also enjoyed simple things, like going out for beers with my brother at one of the local bars where I was almost certain to see childhood friends. One night, I went out for a drink with my brother, and one of my former high school students came over to our booth to talk with Sean, said hello to me, but without any sign of recognition that she knew me. She sat down next to him, chatted away with Sean for about 15 minutes and then asked him: "How is Andy doing?" Sean, grinned, gestured to me and said, "Why don't you ask him?" She really didn't believe him at first - didn't believe it was possible. She had never seen me with an army style haircut, army issue glasses and a mustache.

I was also planning to spend time enjoying the solitude of the cabin on my very rural 30 acres of woodland. But, deer season was on and while I had always previously enjoyed deer hunting, I did not enjoy it that year. In fact, it would be a few years before I would enjoy hunting again. I was in no mood to be disturbed and I remember fiercely chasing the deer hunters off the land, screaming like a mad man as I ran out the door of the cabin shouting at them to get the hell out of there. It wasn't until the following summer, after I'd been discharged, that I was really able to enjoy the cabin and its surrounding woods.

The time passed quickly and all too soon. I headed off to report on December 15 at Fort Devens, Massachusetts, where I was to be stationed for my last six months of Army duty.

Chapter 9
Back in the World - sort of - Ft. Devens, Mass

All too soon, I had to leave my family and report to the 595th Medical Company in Ft. Devens, Massachusetts where I was to serve the last 6 months of my active duty. Ft. Devens was located several miles west of the city of Lowell (about 60 miles west of Boston) in a rural and very beautiful section of Massachusetts. In reading his letters, I know that a century earlier Eugene Kingman had spent time in Lowell training at Camp Chase shortly after he entered the Union Army. While I don't believe Camp Chase was the predecessor to Ft. Devens (Camp Chase was located on the Fair Grounds), there has been a military presence in the area for a long time. At the time I was there, Ft. Devens was the home base for a Special Forces unit and included a large Army hospital.

I didn't like my time there, but I didn't really hate it - and it certainly wasn't a bad situation. Drawing on my Vietnam skills, I was assigned to the hospital pharmacy. But it was boring work essentially consisting of filling pill vials and individual containers for dispensing to patients. In Vietnam I had been involved in the entire medical process; here I was just a pill counter and prescription filler. These activities had no connection to patient's illnesses and I had enjoyed that connection in Vietnam. There I diagnosed an illness, prescribed a treatment and, when it succeeded, felt rewarded. While I hated being in Vietnam, I could find some redemption in my work. This was not true at Ft. Devens. Coupled with that was the fact that I just couldn't wait to get out of uniform. I wanted out of the Army. I wanted to rejoin my old world and resume building my life as well as rebuilding a career.

My duty was not strenuous, workdays went from 8AM to 5 PM with occasional weekend duty. But we didn't draw K-P duty and there was no guard duty in the evenings. We had semiprivate quarters that were out of the way and so no one bothered us with inspections. When I wasn't on duty I could change into civilian clothing and go off base at will and since I had my car there I did so very frequently. There were even trout streams nearby and so I did a little trout fishing that Spring. I had a few friends who lived in the Boston area (an easy trip) and I could get down to NYC on a three-day weekend pass, whenever I could wrangle one - which was fairly often. All of that semi-civilian activity helped me to begin to regain a sense of my prior existence even as I remained in the Army.

At Ft. Devens, I started to shed some of my ingrained habits and some reflexes that I didn't even know I had, from the year in Vietnam. There were things that had been burned into my brain that weren't left behind when I got off the plane and so many of them appeared in strange ways before I was finally able to abandon them. Certain reflexes were deeply imbedded in me as in many Vietnam vets, and those reflexes (reactions to certain stimuli) were only purged over time. One of my abiding memories is of that bus ride from the airport to Ft. Lewis immediately after I arrived on the flight from Vietnam when the bus passed out of the gates of the airport along a highway that had a great deal of overgrowth very close to it. The sound of helicopters, particularly Hueys, brought a knot to my stomach and reminded me of where I had so recently been. (The distinctive sound of a Huey still haunts me thirty years later.)

Parts of the hospital complex, including the hospital pharmacy where I was assigned, were housed in World War II era buildings detached from the hospital itself. I remember walking with three other enlisted men down a long hall connecting two of the old World War II-style wooden buildings at Ft. Devens when suddenly, and without warning, a door slammed shut behind us with a thundering crash. The two of us who had been in Vietnam found ourselves flat on the floor looking foolishly at each other while the other two soldiers were looking at us with puzzled expressions on their faces. They asked us what the hell was going on. Looking at each other in total comprehension and feeling like fellow conspirators, we said, *"Well, you probably wouldn't understand."*

That habit of hitting the ground at loud noises was a hard one to lose; four years later, the reflex was still there. By then I was back in New York and had a loft in Staten Island, not far from the Kill Van Kull. One evening I was sitting there reading when there was a tremendous explosion across the Kill from a gasoline storage tank fire. Before I could even think about it, I found myself flat on the floor as close to the wall as I could get - and feeling foolish. But in that case, there was no one to witness my action!

My time in the pharmacy at Ft. Devens only lasted about six months (although it didn't pass rapidly enough to suit me at the time) giving me an ideal decompression and readjustment period. I don't know how I would have handled my life if I had come back from Vietnam and was dumped immediately back into civilian life. With hindsight, the time at Ft. Devens was a good transition from Vietnam back into the world. At the time , I didn't think I needed a transition from Vietnam but I probably wouldn't have handled it well, even though, as one of the lucky ones who hadn't seen any nasty combat, I didn't have any major demons to purge from my system. Other Vietnam vets, dumped back into "the world" and into a civilian life that had no relationship to the existence that they had become acclimated to in Vietnam naturally had severe problems adjusting.

The reflexive actions they had mastered were those that most soldiers participating in a war have internalized.

In November, about the time I got back from Vietnam, Lt. William Calley went on trial for the massacre at My Lai. The resulting revelations of horribly brutal, almost unthinkable acts, pushed public opinion of the American Vietnam veterans to a very low point, and made many of us associated with the Army deeply ashamed to have been a part of the war. Not only was the war already broadly unpopular at that time, but, as a result of the trial, the picture of the US Army in Vietnam now seemed filled entirely with monsters. Already many of those monsters had come home and so people treated them with wariness or even open hostility. I began to completely avoid mentioning my association with the Army or Vietnam on any of the several long weekend passes I managed to secure that enabled me to go to New York. One of the main reasons many of us returning from Vietnam were confused about our participation in the war effort (often without knowing it) was because we received conflicting, often negative signals from the society we were reentering.

In April, I got a wonderfully supportive letter from my old friend Joe Bresnan. It was one of the few "welcome home" expressions that I received other than from my family. Having known Joe since my first semester in college, we had remained very close friends after college, so his letter was very important to me. In that letter, containing news of recent (and very sad) family problems, but also expressing his delight in the developing relationship with the woman who would soon become his wife, Joe wrote regarding my plans and our relationship:

...When last I saw you, you spoke of spending some time in N.Y.C. When you get out. Are you still considering staying here?

We will have to discuss landing you a job in Monuments (Joe was the Assistant Director of Monuments, in the Parks Department of the City of New York at the time.) if you want one - N.Y.C. Is in pretty strange shape these days - but I think we can wrangle something. Temporary or long-term, I'm all for it.

...I think of you often and wonder when your overlong absence will come to an end.

You may well be angered at my lack of writing, but I simple can't get it all together. I don't know what I would ask you or what I would say. I consider you too close a friend to require much explanation in any case.

It shouldn't be too long for you now. We ought to get in some deep sea fishing during late summer and fall. Get some fresh air!...

(Letter from Joe Bresnan to the author, dated April 8, 1971)

As Joe so painfully, and poignantly, acknowledged in this letter, the gap between those of us who had gone to Vietnam and those who hadn't gone created a gulf that required some patient rebuilding of relationships. Happily, Joe and I rebuilt those emotional bonds, and our friendship has endured all these years. But that was rare. Other relationships dissolved because of the chasm created by Vietnam. Former friends, previously some very close friends, disappeared or drifted away because our paths had diverged so much during those years. Vietnam was the great emotional and social divide for my generation. Feelings about the war were raw and misunderstandings occurred on both side of the divide. Rational or reasoned dialogues were frequently impossible because there was no shared experience about Vietnam and there was no longer a shared set of values - so it seemed.

A couple of stories from those last few months working in the pharmacy of the Army hospital at Ft. Devons are worth telling, as they seem to symbolize some of the attitudes prevalent towards the war and Vietnam.

The first tale from this period involves one of my first attempts at finding a teaching position after the Army. It took place during a job interview while I was still in the Army. While in retrospect I can laugh about the event, it was not at all funny at the time it happened. It illustrates some of the social tensions and the suspicions that the Vietnam War engendered in American society at the time.

My interview took place at a small liberal arts college that will remain unnamed, outside of Philadelphia. The then current occupant of the position had been a classmate of mine in graduate school who was moving. He had enthusiastically recommended me for the position. I traveled to the college at their invitation. I had several excellent references from other professors that enhanced the recommendation of my friend, so I went into the interview with every expectation that things would go well.   And, in the beginning stages it did go very well.   I passed my initial interviews with the various faculty and the Dean with ease. Everything was going swimmingly until I had my final interview which was with the President of the College. That conversation started off on a very good level and stayed there until our luncheon conversation, whereupon the President made some remark about an issue (I don't even remember what it was) and asked me how I felt about it. The issue was a minor one, and I made an off hand remark to the effect of: "Well, I wasn't crazy about that, but it wasn't anything that I would start a march over." With that he stiffened, stared at me carefully - and the interview went down hill before slowly petering out. We finished lunch in virtual silence. I knew something had gone terribly wrong, but I didn't have a clue. Needless to say, I didn't get the job and only later learned that the College had recently had some very violent student marches protesting the Vietnam War at the college, and so the President was not going to hire anyone who might even be remotely considered capable of inciting or organizing a protest march. Certainly not a Vietnam veteran!

The second tale, is based on brief notes that I made about some of the conversations overheard in the pharmacy. Those conversations contain elements of the Army pathology common at the time, and also some mythology about Vietnam common at the time. There is more than just a funny story here. It reflects American attitudes about the Vietnamese war - in words that still haunt me.

The Ft. Devens pharmacy was under the command of an overweight and decidedly out-of-shape US Army Major in his late 30's or early 40's. He spent as little time on the job as possible, delegating most of the work to a harried Lieutenant, who in turn, depended on a very competent Specialist 7 and a civilian employee to actually run the pharmacy. These two people were the ones who provided the pharmacy most of the much needed working professionalism and expertise.

The Major (I referred to him as "Major Howdy-Howdy" because of his habit of answering the phone with a loud, cheery "Howdy, Howdy") had a passion for hunting, fishing and bowling and spent as much of his time at the local rod and gun club as possible. At work, he spent most of his time on the phone or, with his feet propped up on the desk, shooting the breeze with the Lt. or with other friends. Two topics obsessively dominated 90% of all his conversations on the phone or face to face. The first topic was hunting and fishing (really shooting and killing since numbers of animals killed or fish kept was the most important thing to him.) The second topic was Vietnam. While hunting, fishing and bowling were his escape from the drudgery of the pharmacy and the Army, Vietnam was his dark obsession Being sent there was his primary fear. Orders sending him to Vietnam was his recurring nightmare.

Neither Major Howdy-Howdy nor the Lt. had been to Vietnam, but they talked about it all the time and fantasized about what it might be like there. He and the Lt. would spend hours sitting at their desks, in the rear of the pharmacy, drinking coffee or cokes and talking in very loud voices about Vietnam. I spent most of my days in jobs disliked by the others in the pharmacy, but ones I volunteered to handle like weighing out doses of medicines, filling vials, or counting pills. I had discovered early on that they didn't pay any attention to me if I filled the appropriate number of vials of cough syrup, or bottles of pills and kept the inventory current. As a result, I could take very long coffee breaks. I even read on the job since no one really cared as long as the agreed upon amount of work got done. These tasks also kept me in the back of the pharmacy out of sight but within easy hearing distance of the Major's desk, even if they hadn't talked so loudly, and so I overheard far too many inane conversations.

Major Howdy-Howdy spent one particularly inane afternoon in the pharmacy talking very loudly to one of his buddies, a Lt. Colonel in the hospital supply section about one of their fellow officers who had just received orders to go to Vietnam.

Amused, appalled and disgusted by their conversation that day, I made notes on the conversation that survived all these years and were discovered when I dug into my files. While they are, in no way a verbatim record of the conversation, they accurately reflect the essence of the conversation and my (angry) reaction to it. They read like this:

>Today he (Howdy-Howdy) has been trapped at his desk by an even fatter Lt. Colonel and, always one to seize the opportunity to impress his superiors, Howdy-Howdy held forth on Vietnam. Since the Lt. Colonel hadn't been there he was on safe ground and could indulge in considerable fantasizing.
>
>"Yes Sir, if Mary hadn't had the miscarriage with our first attempt, I would have been in Special Forces. Hell, I've always enjoyed banging around you know! Hell, I like opening a can of C's (C-rations) for chow and sacking out on the ground. If I weren't married, I wouldn't mind going over there and cruising around doing a little hunting - you know, riding around shooting a few dinks now and then!"
>
>And then - switching topics without missing a beat - Howdy-Howdy went on with his inane conversation - discussing last night's adventure at the Post Bowling Alley:
>
>"....By god, I'd put her right in the pocket and still get a split! I'd take a step left, a step right - a step back and I'd still get splits! Do you know how many I had? Twenty-nine! By God! Twenty-nine splits!....

My notes captured the essence of his conversations which poured forth in a torrent of words, repeated day after day after day. Along with the conversations, I recorded my thoughts to those absolutely inane conversations showing my utter frustration and simmering anger :

> "Yes, indeed Howdy-Howdy. Fucking eh! And I know from the way you talk that you have a wall full of trophies. Doing a little hunting in Vietnam would be right up your alley - but then again, you wouldn't like it because sometimes the dinks might shoot back. And you wouldn't like it because Vietnam smells like shit. All kinds of shit. Bull shit, dog shit, bird shit, pig shit - but mostly human shit. Fresh shit, stale shit, moist shit and dry shit - but mostly burning shit mixed with diesel fuel around the American Army. You can always tell when you are around an American Army base because it smells like burning shit. The Vietnamese are more practical - they put it to good use on their crops. Our shit is wasted."

A few days before I was discharged from the Army, Major Howdy-Howdy called a special meeting of all the people in the pharmacy to discuss a major problem he had just discovered - the pharmacy's coke fund (our soda fund) was short 35 cents! Because of the magnitude of that problem, he raged on for almost an hour, grilling each of us in turn, trying - in vain - to bully one of us into admitting having neglected to pay for a single can of coke. And so, with those words and that voice ringing my ear and providing my last memory of the Army, I passed back into the world as a civilian - relatively unscathed. Free at last - but feeling like I had emerged from a bad dream.

			DAY	MONTH	YEAR
			9	Jul	69

				DAY	MONTH	YEAR
LB #71 Belmont, NY 14813	Fort Devens, MA 01433	EFFECTIVE DATE	8	Jul	71
30 71 43 109		TYPE OF CERTIFICATE ISSUED: NONE

11a. TYPE OF TRANSFER OR DISCHARGE: Transferred to USAR
b. REASON AND AUTHORITY: Sec VI Ch 2 AR 635-200 SPN 201
c. CHARACTER OF SERVICE: HONORABLE
15. REENLISTMENT CODE: RE-3

12. LAST DUTY ASSIGNMENT AND MAJOR COMMAND: FIRST UNITED STATES ARMY
Med Co USAH Fort Devens, MA 01433

13. DISTRICT, AREA COMMAND OR CORPS TO WHICH RESERVIST TRANSFERRED: USAR CON GP (ANL TNG) USAAC 9700 PAGE BLVD ST LOUIS MO 63132

14. TERMINAL DATE OF RESERVE/UMT&S OBLIGATION: 8 Jul 75

19. GRADE, RATE OR RANK: PV1

20. PLACE OF ENTRY INTO CURRENT ACTIVE SERVICE: Buffalo, NY

STATEMENT OF SERVICE:
	YEARS	MONTHS	DAYS
NET SERVICE THIS PERIOD	2	0	0
OTHER SERVICE	0	0	0
TOTAL	2	0	0
TOTAL ACTIVE SERVICE	2	0	0
FOREIGN AND OR SEA SERVICE	0	11	4

18. PRIOR REGULAR ENLISTMENTS: NONE

HOME OF RECORD AT TIME OF ENTRY INTO ACTIVE SERVICE:
114 S. Main Street
Almond, NY 14804

23. SPECIALTY NUMBER & TITLE: 91 B 20 Medical Sp
RELATED CIVILIAN OCCUPATION AND D.O.T. NUMBER: 2-42 Hosp Attendant

24. DECORATIONS, MEDALS, BADGES, COMMENDATIONS, CITATIONS AND CAMPAIGN RIBBONS AWARDED OR AUTHORIZED:
BRONZE STAR MEDAL; ARMY COMMENDATION MEDAL; PURPLE HEART MEDAL; GOOD CONDUCT MEDAL; VIETNAM CAMPAIGN MEDAL WITH "60-" DEVICE; VIETNAM SERVICE MEDAL; ONE OVERSEAS BAR; NATIONAL DEFENSE SERVICE MEDAL.

25. EDUCATION AND TRAINING COMPLETED:
RVN TNG   MEDICAL CORPSMAN 10 Weeks 1969
ATP 21-111
CODE OF CONDUCT
CRCE A MIL JUSTICE
GENEVA CONV
CBR TNG
INFIL CRSE

27a. INSURANCE IN FORCE: ☐ YES ☒ NO
AMOUNT OF ALLOTMENT: NA
MONTH ALLOTMENT DISCONTINUED: NA

29. SERVICEMEN'S GROUP LIFE INSURANCE COVERAGE: ☒ $15,000 ☐ $10,000 ☐ $5,000 ☐ NONE

26. NON PAY PERIODS TIME LOST (Preceding Two Years): NONE
28. DAYS ACCRUED LEAVE PAID: 17
VA CLAIM NUMBER: NONE

30. REMARKS:
BLOOD GROUP: O POSITIVE
CIVILIAN EDUCATION: 18 Years
Ref ITEM 22C: VIETNAM 6 DEC 69 - 10 NOV 70
Para 9, AR 601-210 Applies.

My D.D.214 - 0r offical dischange
from active duty.

Chapter 10 Reflections

As I write this in early 2004, with the situation in Iraq entering a new and difficult phase, the public is asking for a clarity of our mission there and in Afganistan. In view of those events perhaps it is safe to say that as a nation, we should have had that clarity about our role in Vietnam, but we didn't and I think we paid a heavy price for our failure to develop a clear objective.   And, I think that perhaps we didn't have to develop a clear objective in Vietnam because we had the luxury of a draft that made it possible to send a seemingly endless supply of men off to do their duty (whatever that was). But, because the world had changed so dramatically by 1965, that assumption proved false. So an increasingly reluctant conscript army was sent into a situation where there was no clarity of purpose. We are still debating the effects on the country.

Because the country was so politically divided, both during and after the war, the public portrayal of the Vietnam veteran was almost always conflicted: to those on the ideological left, you were the defender of the many of the very worst attitudes that they were striving to eradicate from American politics, and to those on the right the Vietnam veterans were the ultimate heroes, ready to sacrifice in defense of our country. After the disaster of the interview described in the previous chapter, it was clear that I needed to find my own personal answers to the questions of: a) whether I should take pride in my service or, b) whether I should be ashamed at having served at all! I couldn't figure it out so I quickly became the soldier who never was to my colleagues, friends and family.

My service in the Army and particularly in Vietnam was honorable, but not heroic.   Most of the stories of individuals

Two boys

who served in the armed forces are, like mine, modest, even mundane, stories that remain untold. These "less than heroic experiences" (the reality for the majority of those men and women who served in the armed forces) are very rarely recorded, and even more rarely examined. However, I think examining their stories gives us a better understanding of our collective heritage since that is what our nation's history is about: the combined efforts and sacrifices of men and women who simply did their job and carried out the responsibilities whether they were large or small, simple or complex. I decided that I wanted to examine my story and that I didn't want my story to be subsumed in that great morass of myth - both positive and negative. I didn't want my children (and hopefully) grandchildren to simply say: "Oh yes, he was a Vietnam Veteran, " leaving me to be defined by myth and misunderstanding.

I should mention that I am one of the last generation of American citizen soldiers. That is to say, I am one of the last of those who served because of conscription. Conscription was not unique to the Vietnam War, it provided soldiers in the Civil War, in World Wars 1 and II, and the Korea War. But, by the Gulf War of 1991 things changed. Professional soldiers are now serving and our entire military and its relationship with society has changed. (That only dawned on me after I had devoted many long hours to the creation of this book.) But, while the military clearly prefers the change, whether it will be good for our society remains an unanswered question.

Other Veterans

In doing some research while writing this, I was somewhat surprised to discover that not just American Vietnam veterans faced a public deeply ambivalent about their role after the war.

The American involvement in what we call the Vietnam War was only a small portion of a much longer war called the War of Liberation by the Vietnamese. Peace finally came to Vietnam in the spring of 1975 when Saigon fell. The best estimates indicate some 4 million Vietnamese were killed or wounded in the various stages of the conflict.

To my surprise, veterans of the victorious North Vietnamese army, returning home after the fall of Saigon in April of 1975, also faced a populace and a bureaucracy distrustful of them. In a novel, entitled *The Sorrow of War*, the author, Bao Ninh, a veteran of the war, writes about the reception he faced:

> *In truth he had been deliriously happy to return home to Hanoi when the war ended. He had spent more than three days traveling on the trans-Vietnam "Unification" troop train after the fall of Saigon. It was a happy feeling, and some soldiers now regarded it as the best days of their army life. Still there had been some pain even then.*
>
> *The train was packed with wounded demobilized soldiers....*
>
> *At the start there had been a common emotion of bitterness. There had been no trumpets for the victorious soldiers, no drums, no music. That might have been tolerated, but not the disrespect shown them. The general population just didn't care about them. Nor did their own authorities....*
>
> *The authorities checked the soldiers time after time, searching them for loot. Every pocket of their knapsacks had been searched as though the mountain of property that had been looted and hidden after the takeover of the South had been taken only by soldiers....*

(From The Sorrow of War by Bao Ninh, copyright 1995 by Bao Ninh. Used by permission of Panethon Books, a division of Random House, Inc.)

It seems that, if you survived the War, even on the winning side, it is still difficult to come home.

While only a very small portion of Eugene Kingman's letters and diary entries have been incorporated into my narrative, Eugene was a constant presence as as I remembered and wrote. We are individuals in dramatic contrast. Eugene's letters, and the person who emerged from them, became a mirror in which I examined my own experience. As with many men and women who entered the armed services, my experiences had a very profound and unanticipated life-altering effect on me, as, I am convinced, they did for Eugene although in an entirely different fashion.

I often wonder what really happened to Eugene, who went off to war at 17, a youth without an eduction or a direction in life? We do know very little bit about Eugene's life after the war and that is entirely from family lore. From his war letters, I am convinced that he thought the war would give him a purpose and help him become a man. It probably did both, but after it was over, did it ever become clear to him that he had paid a price? He had indeed become a man but his idealism was gone, replaced by cynicism. Was that why he decided that he was now beyond college? He wrote frequently of going to college for the first two years of his service and then, after Port Hudson, he wrote to Charlie to say a college education was no longer a goal. It just vanished from his letters. I can only think that his experiences were so life altering that he felt college was no longer desirable. He had accomplished many goals, he had fought in his crusade, and had become a leader (in his eyes) with his promotion to Sergeant. He had undergone the rite of passage becoming an adult. So for him to have returned to college probably seemed to be a step backward, to return to a stage of adolescence.

After all, he had been a Sergeant and had commanded others under some difficult and harrowing times. Why would he have wanted to become a humble student? And, seen from his perspective, you have to ask, why indeed?

After reading his letters, I believe that unrealized personal aspirations and his stunning realization in understanding that the reality of war was a less than a heroic endeavor (even in a war fought for good and noble intentions) left Eugene in an embittered state of mind that subsequently influenced the remainder of his life. If the family tales are to be believed, Eugene had all his youthful dreams, aspirations and hopes dashed and found war to be humbling, nasty and brutish. It would seem, that he saw the worst in his fellow men and so after the war, turned inward on himself, pulling away from the world.

I've often thought about him as I reflected on my own life after Vietnam. I've also wondered why Eugene's story went untold for almost one hundred and twenty years until my mother put his letters in print. Certainly Eugene's experiences and his service were honorable, but seemingly not heroic in the eyes of his contemporaries. As a result, it took more than a century for his story to be told. Was there little interest in his story because there were so many veterans of the Civil War around and it seemed that we knew everything we needed to know about them? (And, correspondingly, about the war itself?) I think so. But perhaps it was also because he didn't care to tell his story and was content to have it live on in family lore and in the shadows of the myth of the Civil War. Or, perhaps, he simply didn't want to relive his experiences by retelling them.

In contrast to Eugene my service in the Army (and particularly in Vietnam) turned out to have had an entirely unanticipated

Eugene Kingman
I read with great sympathy Eugene's last diary entries where he remained sick and emotionally spent but still in the thick of the action, until the absolute end of his term - and then a few days more!

"Tuesday 15. Our time is out today and yet we are not discharged. We may go by the 20th of the month.

Wednesday, November 16, 1864. Our Regt. went out with the Forage train today. We did not get in until dark. Gone all day. It has been a very pleasant day.

Thursday 17. Quite warm and pleasant - not much of importance going on today.

Friday, November 18, 1864. We have got our orders! Go home. We shall probably go tomorrow morning. It is very rainy.

Saturday, 19. This morning we started and marched to Winchester where we caught the train and then we came to Martinsburg, a march

of 27 miles. It has been a pleasant day, but it rains tonight. It is just a month from our last battle.

Sunday, November 20, 1864. Got aboard the cars this morning and have come on to Baltimore where we are now stopping in the Soldiers Rest. We came in box cars. It has been rainy and cold all day. We arrived about 8 o'clock and have just eaten a good supper.

Tuesday, November 22, 1864 Started last night in the cars for New York. We came through the night and are now stopping at the Park Barracks. We expect to leave on a Fall River boat this afternoon.

Wednesday 23. I am at home. We came through to Fall River last night on the boat and then took the cars for Boston arriving at daybreak this morning.... Then I left and came on home to New Glouchester. At home after a long absence.

Thursday, November 24, 1864 At home thanksgiving day. Just the right time. I am a lucky man.
(Vintage, pgs 329 and 330)

Eugene was just 20. But, he had survived and was home.

and unforseen influence on my subsequent life and career. When I got to Vietnam, I immersed myself in the work of the dispensary and (much to my surprise) enjoyed working with the men I worked with and found considerable satisfaction in doing the work. I enjoyed serving others in a healing situation, and, in contrast to my previous life as an artist, where the forcus was on 'ME," in Vietnam I focused on being part of a team and on those I was treating. In contrast to Eugene, who wanted to be recognized by others, including his siblings, his peers and his parents and become an officer or hero (or both), my expectations were much more modest. I went to Vietnam simply wanting to survive and keep my own sense of having done the best I could. When I got there and found that serving others, whether they were fellow soldiers or Vietnamese civilians was satisfying and rewarding in itself, I found satisfaction in doing so. Unlike Eugene, I neither sought, nor received any adulation for my activities.

Eugene wrote home with great enthusiasm about the exotic landscape, the sights and new experiences he discovered or experienced during the more than two years he spent in Louisiana, but they must have disappeared from his mind later in life. It seems that he never revisited Louisiana, the South, (or even the Shenandoah Valley), nor did he seem to have any eagerness to do so. In contrast, my less than ideal introduction to Asia with its magnificant landscapes, peoples and culture made me eager to return and to learn more about it, and luckily, I have had ample opportunity to do so. Having said that, I must also say, I've not returned to Vietnam.

Looking back with thirty years hindsight, it's vividly clear that even though I certainly would have preferred to spend the time in another way, the Army and my Vietnam experience had a extraordinary profoundly positive influence on me. My induction into the Army was particularly traumatic, and I just hated most aspects of it. (As my letters clearly indicated!) However, when I entered the Army (dispite my six years spent attending college in that most cosmopolitan of cities, New York) I remained, in my attitudes and understanding of the world, a country boy from a small town. Service in Vietnam made me understand that I was part of a much larger and more complex world, although at the time I was not consciously aware of it. However, I should be very clear in saying that Vietnam was no fun. (For the most part, I certainly didn't enjoy being there and at times deeply resented it.) I also discovered I was very interested in a larger world than I had previously known and, additionally, had become fascinated by my glimpses of other cultures! My time in Vietnam - whether out on Medcaps, working in the dispensary, visiting Hue or on my Japanese R & R, along with the emerging realization of how different was the Asian cultural view of life (and art) - made me eager to learn more about that (still) distant and exotic part of the world and the people and cultures there. So later in my subsequent career in higher education, when I was given the opportunity to travel and work with people from other cultures, I eagerly did so and have been amply rewarded.

Finally, one of the most profound things I learned in Vietnam was the role luck (or chance) plays in our lives. I learned about humility and about the arbitrary nature of life in many ways that I had not previously understood. Things will happen to us that we can't and don't understand. We will all remain subject to fate. Among other things, I think about how, had the person or people setting up the 122's adjusted the aiming sticks slightly differently on several occasions, I would not be writing this today. It is a humbling thought, but one that, if remembered, keeps the travails of life in perspective and reminds one where we all stand.

On the other hand, I also learned that great opportunities for personal growth, learning and new insights present themselves in unanticipated ways. It is up to the individual to take advantage of them - or not! I learned about making the most of those moments that arise in one's life in unanticipated ways that gave me both very profound insights and opportunities. In some very basic ways, the insights I found in one blinding moment on the runway in Phu Bai and in those all-too-brief seven days spent on my R & R in Japan, gave me more insights into art and culture than had my entire education up to that point.

And so, this examination of my brief time, more than three decades ago, of the two years of my Army experience, has led me to conclude that my experience in the Army and, most importantly, my time in Vietnam were, in retrospect, probably some of the most defining years of my life.

About the author

After his discharge in 1971, Andrew Phelan returned to New York City where he accepted a position at the Pratt Institute, a professional art, design and architecture school, where he remained in various faculty and administrative positions for almost twenty years. In the early 1980's he was appointed by then Mayor, Edward Koch, as a member of the New York Vietnam Veterans Commission. While on the Commission he served on the Monument Selection Subcommittee and as Chair of the Jury for the design of the New York City Vietnam Veteran's Memorial. Since 1992 he has lived in Norman, Okalahoma where he is Professor and Director of the School of Art at the University of Oklahoma. For his service in Vietnam he was awarded, among others, the Purple Heart, Bronze Star and Army Commendation medals.

Acknowledgments

I would like to gratefully acknowledge the contributions I have received from a number of individuals and institutions who have generously assisted in the making of this book. First, I would like to thank my mother, Helene Phelan and my sister Elizabeth Myers, as well as Sue Turner for saving my letters. Without the letters there would never have been a book.

I would also like to thank the University of Oklahoma Research Council for their support in giving me a small grant that helped with the design of this book, enabling me to use the extraordinarily talented designer, Lei Cai, who helped design a book suitable for the two stories. Additionally, I am deeply indebted in another way to my mother Helene Phelan who graciously allowed me to use material from her book, *Tramping Out the Vintage,* the edited letters and diaries of Eugene Kingman. His story, and her efforts to tell it, played an important part in my decision to create a book based on my letters, and I believe the use of Eugene's letters adds immeasurably to my story. My son, Lucas Phelan, spent many hours scanning in the photographs and letters for which I am very grateful. Also, Danielle Stephens reprinted some of my old negatives that I thought were beyond salvaging.

Others who contributed to the book include a number of individuals who read all or parts of the manuscript, each making valuable suggestions. These include; Mary Margaret Holt, Andrew Horton, Pamela Scofield, Megan Phelan, Steve and Pam Bradford, as well as Joseph and Adrienne Bresnan. Andrew Strout, Victor Koshkin-Youritzin and Ted Herstand, in particular, deserve very special mention and my profound thanks for all the time they devoted to carefully reading the manuscript and for their invaluable suggestions.

My thanks to Pantheon Books, a division of Random House, for permission to use the words of Bao Ninh, and to The Free Press for permission to use Ronald Spector's insightful observation.

In addition to those mentioned, I would also like to offer my thanks to all those who, like Jerry and Wanda Westheimer and Yoshie Good, gave me encouragement to continue with this project.

And finally, but most importantly, I am deeply indebted to, and honored by Jason Yu, who has so generously underwritten and arranged for the publication of this book. Without him, and without his wonderful support, it would never have been more than a manuscript printed in a dozen or so copies.

Selected Bibliography

sources

Edelman, Bernard, editor, *Dear America*, W.W. Norton & Co., New York, 1985, ISBN 0-393-01998-5

Laurence, John, *The Cat From Hue*, Public Affairs, New York, 2002. ISBN 1-58648-160-6

Leepson, Mark, ed. with Helen Hannaford, *Webster's New World Dictionary of the Vietnam War,* Simon & Schuster, Inc., New York, 1999, ISBN 0-02-862746-6

Ninh, Bao, *The Sorrow of War,* Pantheon Books, New York (translated from the Vietnamese by Phan Thanh Hao and edited by Frank Palmos) 1993, ISBN 0-679-43961-7

Nolan, Keith W., *Ripcord, Screaming Eagles Under Seige, Vietnam 1970*, Presido Press, Novato, CA, 2000, ISBN 0-89141-642-0

Phelan, Helene, editor, *Tramping Out The Vintage*, Phelan, Almond, NY, 1983. ISBN: 0-9605836-4-5

Santoli, Al, *Everything We Had*, Ballantine Books, New York, 1981, ISBN 0-345-32279-7

Spector, Ronald H., *After Tet*, Vintage Books, New York, 1994, ISBN: 0-679-75046-0

Summers, Harry G., *The Vietnam War Almanac*, Presido Press, Novato, CA, 1985, ISBN 0-89141-692-7

Stanton, Shelby L., *The Rise and Fall of An American Army*, Dell, New York, 1985, ISBN: 0-440-20031-8